BUILDING
DATABASES

Using Microsoft Access 2010

F. Mark Schiavone, Ph.D.

Sycamore Technical Press
www.sycamoretechnicalpress.com

Preface

Microsoft Access is a powerful database management system. It provides easy-to-work-with tools to assist you in the creation of sophisticated databases which may include forms for data entry and management and reports for list or summary views of your data.

I've worked with Microsoft Access since its earliest implementation, and over the years have expanded to working with database servers such as Microsoft SQL Server, Oracle, and MySQL. Having dealt with the major database applications I still see many instances in the workplace where a database constructed in Microsoft Access perfectly suits the organization's needs.

This book, and indeed, the *Building* series arose as a result of my observations when creating training materials for large organizations. At the time, software books tended to focus on inventories of all the menu commands and buttons you could choose and did little to address the day to day needs of the harried modern office worker. Staff weren't impressed with the comprehensive knowledge of the trainer (or author) as much as being impressed when, in the training environment, they ran across someone who knew how to help them get to the procedures they needed to know *now* in order to complete some project or task back at their desk.

Thus, this book traces its heritage to earlier versions designed to be delivered in the context of workplace training. Then as now, the approach is to identify and focus on the most important tasks required to get a specific job done. It is my sincere wish that upon completion of this material you'll find that such a task-based focus will leave you with the skills required to design a reliable and easy to use database.

Manual Conventions

Throughout this manual reference is made to various components of the software. Tabs, ribbons, groups, command buttons, and named views and windows appear in boldface type, for example, **OK** and **Font**. Keystrokes appear in boldface italic type, for example, ***Ctrl + V*** and ***Enter***. When possible, the words *select* and *choose* have been used in this manual to allow you the option of using either the mouse or keyboard. Throughout this manual you'll find the following helpful items:

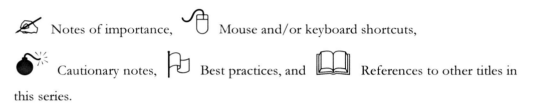 Notes of importance, Mouse and/or keyboard shortcuts, Cautionary notes, Best practices, and References to other titles in this series.

Table of Contents

Introduction

This book is designed to provide the reader with the basic skill set to design and construct a relational database. Although the focus of the book uses Microsoft Access as the development and database managing environment, many of the skills covered are applicable to database design in general. The reader will step through the tasks generally associated with prudent database design – first focusing on developing a conceptual map of how a database should be constructed and then working through the process of formalizing the design. Once the initial database design has been created the book then steps through procedures to create the major objects – in the case of Microsoft Access – these are the tables, queries, forms and reports that constitute a working relational database.

The chapter on table design includes specifying data types, setting indices, applying format masks and validation rules – all with the goal of ensuring that each table efficiently store data and effectively guard against bad or corrupt data. Following the construction of tables, the book covers how to link various tables together to model the two most common scenarios in a relational database: one-to-many, and many-to-many joins.

Following discussion on table design and join types, the reader will learn about different query types – select queries which pull selective data from one or more tables – and action queries which act upon data or the tables in a database. Queries also benefit from various join types between their underlying tables and this topic will also be discussed.

Tables and queries make up the part of a Microsoft Access database which are universally shared with other relational databases. The book will continue however with two important components of a Microsoft Access database that provides significant ease of use to anyone working with a database – forms and reports. For both topics the book reviews the various types of forms and reports and then steps through specific procedures for creating both basic and fairly sophisticated forms and reports. Regarding the latter, grouped reports and reports that automatically summarize or tally numeric data will be covered.

Although this book will show you how to quickly create tables, queries, forms and reports its major focus is to serve as a short primer in database design. Databases have the potential to be fairly complex applications. Dealing with this complexity is far easier if you first design the structure of your database in a thoughtful and considered manner. Once you have a correctly designed database structure, many of Access' wizards can help create the other objects such as data entry forms or summary reports that make your design useful to model real world situations.

Chapter 1 | Overview of Access

This book is a broad overview of the basics of designing a relational database. We'll realize designing a database using Microsoft Access as both the design tool you will use to construct a database, and as the container that you or other uses will use to work with your database and its underlying data. As such, it would be a good start to briefly review the various terms we'll encounter and to step through the basic procedures to create a database file and navigate through the various types of objects associated with a Microsoft Access database.

Database Terminology

Before you begin using Microsoft Access 2010, you need to be familiar with several database terms.

Term	Definition
Database	A collection of information on a single item such as an employee database or a telephone directory. A database is built on *tables*. A *relational* database stores data in tables that permit you to relate one object to many facts (or many objects to many facts).
Table	A collection of *records* arranged in a column and row format. Each column corresponds to one of the *fields* of the table and each row corresponds to an individual *record*. Example: employee information for an organization.
Record	A collection of information about one item in a table. In a table, records are represented as rows. Each record consists of the same set of fields. Example: the information for a specific employee in an organization.
Field	A category of information. In a table, fields are represented as columns. Example: The last name of each employee.
Primary Key	One or more fields that represent a value or set of values that uniquely identifies each record in a table. Primary keys are required if you intend to build a relational database. Good candidates are Social Security Number, Employee ID, or email address.
Foreign Key	One or more fields that match, in data type, the primary key of another table. Tables containing foreign key fields may be joined to primary key-containing tables.
Join	Also called a *relational join*, it is the manner in which tables are related in a database. Typical joins include *one-to-one*, *one-to-many*, and *many-to-many*.
Referential Integrity	In a relational database, this is the capacity of the database to maintain synchronization of the joined tables. Editing or deleting information in one table may cause automatic updates or deletions in related or joined tables.

Opening an Existing Access Database

When you open Access, your first choices are to create a new blank database, create a database from an existing on-line template, or open an existing database. If Access has been used previously up to 4 of the last databases opened will be displayed (by default). If the desired database is not among this list (or the list of recently opened databases), you will need to locate the file using the procedure discussed below.

How to Open an Existing Access Database

Step 1.   From the **Open Recent Database** area, select **More…**.

Step 2.   Navigate to the drive and/or folder containing the desired database.

Step 3.   Choose the appropriate database name and select **Open**.

How to Open an Earlier Version Access Database

If you attempt to open a database which was created in an earlier version of Access, the following dialog box will appear:

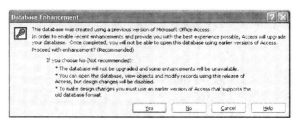

Step 1.   Choose **Yes** to convert the database or choose **No** to open the database with limitations. Selecting **Cancel** will abandon the operation.

Step 2.   If you choose **Yes** in Step 1, you will be prompted to save the converted database. Provide a unique name and/or a unique location for the converted database, and then choose **OK**.

The file extension between former and the current Access versions are different, so it isn't possible to overwrite your original database file when converting it. You can return to the original file if necessary.

Creating a New Database

You can create a new database when you start Access, or from within Access once it is running. A new database is empty of all database objects.

How to Create a New Database

Step 1.   From the **File** tab, choose **New**.

Step 2.   In the **Available Templates** area, choose **Blank Database**.

Step 3.   Enter a file name and/or navigate to the desired drive and/or folder first, then name your database.

Step 4.   Choose **Create**.

 Warning: If you already have a database open when you go to create a new database, the opened database is automatically closed. You will be prompted to save any changed objects.

Understanding the Navigation Pane

When you either create a new database or open an existing database, Access displays the **Navigation Pane** to the left side of the working area. The Navigation Pane replaces the **Database Window** from prior versions of Access. By default, when creating a new database, the Navigation Pane only displays table objects as illustrated below.

If you need to create and/or view other objects, choose the drop down arrow located in the banner area of the Navigation Pane. Select from the options below.

Navigation Pane Components

Component	Description
Navigate to Category	Organizes database objects by custom categories, object type, created or modified dates, etc.
	Custom lists all objects as well as any custom groups you've created to further organize database objects.
	Object Type organizes objects by major predefined types such as tables, queries, forms, reports, and modules. These types correspond to the tabs in the database window from previous versions of Access.
	Tables and Related Views organizes tables and objects such as forms which may be used to manage table data.
	Created Date Arranges by creation date.
	Modified Date Arranges by modification date.
Filter by Group	Drills down to list objects within a specific group, such as tables or reports.
All Access Objects	Lists all objects, grouped by type.

Access Database Objects

A single Access database file is composed of six different types of objects. These objects represent the components used to build and manipulate the database, although not all objects are required for this purpose (for example, macros and modules are used to perform certain actions or contain VBA programming code, respectively, and may not appear in all databases). When you build a database all objects are contained within a single **accdb** file (unless you create a split database, discussed in Appendix B). The descriptions of objects below is a generalized one. As we investigate each object type in more detail other uses will become evident.

Macro and module objects are treated as special objects. Their object type will not appear in the list of All Access Objects until specifically created (from the **Create** tab, **Other** group).

Object	Description
Table	Tables store data in records (rows) and fields (columns), and collectively are the foundation of a database. All queries, forms, and reports display data from the tables in the database.
Query	Queries are questions about the data contained in the database's tables or a request to perform an action on that data. Queries can be based on tables or other queries. The data displayed as a result of a query is a subset of the data contained in the tables.
Form	Forms are used to view, enter, and edit data in fields. Forms can be based on tables or queries. If data is entered or edited in a form, the table information is automatically updated.
Report	Reports are formatted and organized printed output. Reports can be based on tables or queries. The data displayed in a report is the data contained in the tables.
Macro	Macros are sets of one or more predefined actions that can be run from a form or report, or by opening the macro in the Database window. Access macros are not recorded; rather the actions are chosen from a list of choices.
Module	Modules store custom procedures written in the Visual Basic for Applications programming language. The code in a module is only activated if it is called from a form or report.

Overview of Access Ribbons

In Access, all major tasks are grouped into *Ribbons*, which have fundamentally replaced menus in all members of the Microsoft Office suite. **Ribbons** and their attendant **groups** are used to create and modify all database objects as well as to manipulate data.

The first 4 ribbons are always present. The remaining ribbons are context sensitive and appear when you are working with specific objects.

Access Ribbons

Name	Description
Home	Generally manages groups associated with views and data manipulation. Groups include **Views**, **Clipboard**, **Font**, **Rich Text**, **Records**, **Sort & Filter**, and **Find**.
Create	Provides quick access to the manual and wizard-based tools for creation of each of the Access objects: tables, queries, forms, reports, macros and modules.
External Data	Manages tools for the importation and exportation of data. This includes the new functions related to import of data from email surveys and integration with Sharepoint Lists.
Database Tools	Work with Macros, manage relationships, run specific database analysis/report tools and migrate data to SQL server or create a split database.
Table Tools - Datasheet	Visible when working with tables. Change views, alter or edit table structure, manage field data types, and work with table relationships.
Table Tools - Design	Work with tools specific to the design or modification of a table's structure.
Query Tools - Design	Run a query, manage query types, design/alter queries and/or their properties.
Form Design Tools - Design	Displays groups specific to working with designing a form. This includes generalized formatting but also provides access to the rich set of form controls.
Form Design Tools - Arrange	Groups tools useful when working with grouped controls.
Form Design Tools - Format	Provides tools used to manage the overall format of a form, such as font and formatting.
Report Design Tools - Design	Similar to the tools used to design forms.
Report Design Tools - Arrange	Similar to the tools used to arrange controls on a form.
Report Layout Tools - Format	Similar to the form layout tools but includes tools for grouping and totaling data.
Report Layout Tools - Page Setup	Controls to set page size, margins, and paper orientation.
Print Preview	This specialized tab and its related groups appears whenever a database object is viewed in Print Preview mode. Groups to control page layout, zoom levels and exporting to other Microsoft Office applications are provided.

Chapter 2 | Fundamentals of Database Design

Nearly all databases store data in a grid format – each table consisting of columns which denote various attributes (such as last name or city) and rows – which map to individual records. Because this simple grid format is also found in modern spreadsheet applications (such as Microsoft Excel) it's natural for people to use spreadsheets instead of a database to store data. For many reasons this is a bad idea and those who choose the spreadsheet-as-database route soon learn that there are limitations. For example, it's pretty easy to sort a column of data in a spreadsheet only to discover that doing so immediately breaks the relationship between the data in the sorted column and the rest of the grid. This is because a spreadsheet isn't constrained to treat any row of data as if it's related. In a database this would never occur. A row maps formally to an individual record.

Another limitation of the spreadsheet-as-database approach is the complete inability for a spreadsheet to model real-world associations that we'll soon formally discuss: one-to-many and many-to-many relationships. A modern database such as Microsoft Access (and almost all other database management systems) are equipped to easily manage such relationships. You may never have heard of a one-to-many relationship but they're all around you. Think of a household inventory. Each room may have one to many objects within it. A recipe has one to many ingredients and also has one to many procedures. As individuals, we usually have more than one way to contact us – land phone lines, email, cell phones and fax machines all make for a one-to-many relationship between a person and their contact information. Likewise many-to-many relationships are also easily identified. If you think more broadly about a recipe database, it's true that each recipe may have many ingredients and it's just as likely that an individual ingredient, for example, a garlic clove, may be in many recipes. Airline reservation systems are classic examples of many-to-many relationships. Each flight has many passengers and over time, each passenger (which you can think of as a client of the airline) may take many flights. None of these examples can be managed easily within the context of a spreadsheet – only a relational database can effectively model such associations.

To introduce you to the concepts of database design we'll begin with a spreadsheet-based example. Originally created to maintain contact information, you'll see how its initial design begins to fall apart as the ways you can contact a person proliferate. Other problems will arise and all of these will be addressed once we migrate the design from the spreadsheet into a relational database.

Overview of Database Design

Modern databases store information about objects, places, or events in a manner that satisfies the condition that these items may have one or more associated facts. Databases use *relational joins* (also simply called *joins*) to enable the database to efficiently realize these facts of association. Common examples of such situations (and the *relational joins* they embody) include:

- A staff database that relates each staff member to his or her non-native language skills. Each staff member may have no non-native language skills or they may be multi-lingual. This is an example of a *one-to-many* relationship.

- A contact database that stores telephone numbers, fax numbers, and e-mail addresses for each person. Individuals may have only a home phone or they may have many different telephone numbers, fax numbers, and e-mail addresses. Like the example above, this models a *one-to-many* relationship.

- A library catalog database that stores information about books and authors. Each author may be associated with many books and some books may have many authors. This example models a *many-to-many* relationship.

- A course enrollment database that stores information about students and their registered classes. Each student may have one or more classes and each class has one or more students. This is a *many-to-many* relationship.

- A hotel reservation system that stores information about rooms, clients, and room reservations. Each room over time has many client stays and each client may have one or many stays over time. This is a *many-to-many* relationship.

To help illustrate why multiple tables of related information make sense let's examine how trying to use a single table to model a simple real world situation – a contact database – results in numerous problems. We'll show how modeling the same data in a relational database results in a far more elegant solution.

Example: A Contact Database

Many people have an initial difficulty with the concept of multiple tables in a database. After all, it isn't uncommon to use an application such as Microsoft Excel to store data. If they can use a single worksheet to manage their data needs, why migrate to a database application and deal with many tables?

The comparison between a spreadsheet application and a database is a good one. In many cases, modeling relatively simple data works fine in a spreadsheet application such as Excel. At first glance, organized data in a spreadsheet even looks like the same data contained within a database table. Such a simple comparison breaks down as datasets grow either in size or complexity; spreadsheets show their weakness as a data storage tool. We'll illustrate this point by imagining how a simple contact "database", modeled in a spreadsheet, begins to fail as the complexity of the data exceeds the initial design considerations. Following that, we'll rescue this design by modeling it using the relational database design concepts.

Later in this chapter we'll review the significant design steps required to plan a database and discuss the concept of *normalization* which is an approach to database design that, among other goals, strives to reduce redundancy in the data and ensures an efficient, compact design.

Initial Design: Contacts in a Spreadsheet

This initial design would also fail if modeled in a single database table. The example illustrates the problems which arise when modeling some real world situations using a single table or worksheet.

Imagine that you want to store contact information about family and friends and you decide that using something Microsoft Excel would be a good application. You create a new workbook and start naming columns in the first worksheet. Your initial (and greatly simplified) design might look like this:

So you start entering data into your new "database" and things are going well. Not everyone has a work phone or mobile device so some cells end up being empty. You hit your first snag when your Grandmother informs you that she's just installed two fax machines: one in her home office and another one in her car.

If your database is to keep up with accurately tracking contact information, you have little recourse with this design but to add two additional columns: fax1 and fax2 (calling the second column mobile fax would seem silly since only Grandma seems to have one!) Your amended design, along with some sample data, now looks like this:

	A	B	C	D	E	F	G
1	Name	Home Phone	Work Phone	Mobile	E-mail	Fax 1	Fax 2
2	Mom	334-3339		334-3311	mom@gmail.com		
3	Sue	677-9234	869-2200	304-1213	sue@xmail.com		
4	Sam	445-3449	430-7689	430-8891	sam@123.com		
5	Granny	445-0090				445-2424	401-7788
6							

Your database continues to serve you well until the day that your friend Sue calls. The hospital where she works has issued her an additional cell phone and she needs to carry it along with her personal mobile phone. If you need to contact her during her shift you'll need to use the new number. This is bad news. Do you create a seventh column to store this single fact? Perhaps you can store it in the Fax 1 column and hope that you remember that Sue doesn't have a fax – this is her work cell number. You decide for accuracy and resolve to add that seventh column, named Work Mobile (here 7 columns refers to those columns storing contact info for each person – the eight column is Name).

In the example above, the major failure of the design is the way new sets of facts are accommodated. Each new type of contact method requires an additional column. Besides the inelegance of this approach, it brings additional problems, namely:

Many cells are blank – the fax 2 column may have a single entry even though your database grows to hundreds of rows (records). These blank spaces are inefficient as the spreadsheet application (or an actual database) must utilize disk storage even for blank cells or fields.

If you need to look up a record based on a phone number, which column do you search on? The number could map to your Home Phone, Work Phone, Mobile, Work Mobile, Fax 1 or Fax 2 fields. The fact that as the administrator of this database you can't immediately identify the field that contains a given set of data underscores the difficulty with this design.

So how does this situation get fixed by migrating to a relational database management system such as Access?

Improved Design: Normalization of Your Data

The present approach fails a central design tenant of database design. In an efficient and well considered database, each field in a table stores a unique kind of information. In our example we're really dealing with two sets of unique facts: (1) the people who you wish to contact and (2) one or more ways to contact them. Our example fails in that there are multiple columns for specific contact methods even though conceptually they all fall into the same generalized group: ways to contact a person. Although we'll discuss database *normalization* in more detail, the term in this present example means that the current approach is not compact. Despite the number of contact-related columns in our design, conceptually, they all represent the same thing – a contact method.

Our new design will model a classic *one-to-many* relationship that recognizes the real-world fact that for each person there are one to many ways to contact them. To normalize our current design, we'll break the database into two separate tables, representing the two central facts we're trying to capture: (1) people and (2) ways to contact them. In order for a database to be able to relate these two tables together we'll need to bring in an additional concept: primary and foreign keys.

A primary key is a field or a group of fields within a database table that uniquely identifies each row in that table. Primary keys may or may not be present in all tables in a database, but they are required to exist in tables that model the *one* side of a *one-to-many* relationship. In our new design, we'll need a primary key in the table that manages the people we wish to contact. There can be many candidates for a primary key and we'll discuss how to identify primary keys later. For simplicity, we'll use an autonumber field to assign a unique PersonID for each person in our database.

A foreign key is a field located in a table that is on the *many* side of a *one-to-many* relationship. The foreign key field isn't unique – in fact it should not contain unique entries. Its major requirement is that it be of the same *data type* as the primary key field. The purpose of a foreign key is to enable the database to relate the zero to many records on the *many* side with the single, primary key record from the *one* side of the relationship.

So to normalize our failed spreadsheet application we begin by creating a new table that stores the basic facts about each person in our contact database. Our new **Contacts** table might appear as follows:

pk_ID	Name
1	Mom
2	Sue
3	Sam
4	Granny

The field **pk_ID** is the primary key for our *contacts* table. Many database systems supply an auto numbering or auto incrementing field type (usually a numeric data type) that provides the designer with an easy to use primary key. As we enter additional contacts into our table the **pk_ID** field will automatically increment for us.

Our new table isn't much different from the initial approach we used in our spreadsheet – one row for each person. The big difference comes in how the specific contact information is modeled. Recall that we've identified the ways to contact a person as being the second set of facts. At this point we are less concerned about the individual methods of contact and instead focus on a way to identify the method and its specific value. For example *email* and *home phone* identify methods and *mom@gmail* and 334-3339 are specific values for each of these methods. Thus the minimum number of fields our second table needs is three: a foreign key field, used to relate specific records back to our contacts table; a field to identify the method of contact, and a field to identify each value for that method. Populated with the same data that appears in the figure on Page 9 from our inefficient design, our second table, **ContactMethods** would appear as follows:

fk_ID	Method	Value
1	Home Phone	334-3339
1	Mobile	334-3311
1	email	mom@gmail.com
2	Home Phone	677-9234
2	Work Phone	889-2200
2	Mobile	304-1213
2	email	sue@xmail.com
3	Home Phone	445-3449
3	Work Phone	430-7689
3	Mobile	430-8891
3	email	sam@123.com
4	Home Phone	445-0090
4	Fax (Home)	445-2424
4	Fax (Car)	401-7788

Four things should become apparent with this design:

1. The table can elegantly handle any new contact method in the future. It simply becomes a new entry in the Method field.

2. There are no blank fields (or cells if you want to still think in terms of a spreadsheet). The data are efficiently packed into the table.

3. You know exactly where to search this table for any given fact. The types of contact methods are all located in the Method field and specific values (such as a phone number) are all in the Value field.

4. The data in this table aren't particularly *human readable* in that without knowing which person maps to each value in the **fk_ID** field you can't immediately tell which contact method/value belongs to which person.

The latter point may at first seem like a major drawback. Why use a relational database management system if you can't read the data in your tables? The short answer is that users shouldn't be accessing table data directly in a database. Access provides you with powerful form and report design tools and viewing or editing data should be mediated through these objects and not through tables. This is especially true since forms and reports can easily manage the task of pulling data from related tables.

Another potential point of concern: we've created two separate tables from what was originally a single, albeit poorly designed table. How do we connect the tables together? The simple answer is that through good design, we let Access make the connection by using the **Relationships** tool. Once Access has been shown how the two tables relate (here by connecting the pk_ID field from our **Contacts** table to the fk_ID field in the **ContactMethods** table), queries, forms and reports based on this relationship automatically "understand" how to work with the data in the two tables. A shot of the connecting relation link, as rendered in the Relationships tool, is illustrated below.

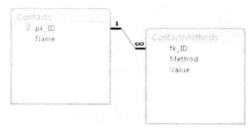

Now that the tables have been linked, creating a form with a related subform is an easy task. To illustrate this point consider the following figure. This form clearly manages the data from our two new tables. The main part of the form pulls data from our **Contacts** table while the subform displays only those related records from the **ContactMethods** table. Such a form may be used to view, edit or create new records. Such an approach removes any worry concerning the readability of table data. Since the relationships were already designed (as illustrated in the previous figure), it took the form wizard a few seconds to pull this form together:

Now that we've had a quick demonstration showing why relational databases manage most real-world data better than a single table design, let's explore database design in more detail.

A Brief Outline of the Database Design Process

Constructing a well-crafted database is very much like constructing a building. If the design is fundamentally sound and well documented the construction process goes smoothly and the result is a usable building. No builder would start work on a 4-story office building without plans. No database designer should attempt to construct a database without first giving thought to the design.

The design process is straightforward. The major tasks are outlined below and then individually discussed in more detail. The design process can frequently be reiterative in that as the plan develops, it may be necessary to jump back a few tasks and rework the design.

Tasks in the Database Design Process

To construct a database, a developer follows a multi-step process.

Task 1.   Determine the overall needs of the database and identify the major categories of objects, places, or events that the database will recognize.

Task 2.   Design the tables that will store the basic facts about the items identified in Task 1. In general, each class of object, place or event will map to a single table. As the design process moves forward, especially during the process of *normalization*, it will frequently be the case that additional tables are added to the design.

Task 3.   For each proposed table, assign potential *primary keys*. This is especially important for any table that models data on the *one* side of a relational join. For tables that will store the *many* facts about an object, place, or event (i.e., the table will be on the *many* side of a *relational join*) assign *foreign keys* as well.

Task 4.   Ensure that each proposed table is *normalized*, which is a process that ensures that tables will be compact and efficient. Improper normalization will cause problems and will result in a poorly designed database.

Task 5.   Formalize the *relational joins* by constructing table joins.

We will review each of these tasks in detail in the following sections.

Task 1. Determining the Overall Needs

This task is as much art as it is science. In determining the needs, you attempt to map out some real-world process into an overall database design. Most database designers follow these basic steps:

Step 1.   Identify the key objects, places, or events that the database will model. For each object, place, or event, further identify facts that can potentially be modeled as *one-to-many* or *many-to-many* relationships. For example, if you need to track staff and their skills, both staff information and their skills resolve to separate tables. Further, staff to staff skills is a one-to-many relationship as each staff may have few or many associated skills.

Step 2. Map out on paper the lists of objects, places, or events you will be working with. Include any cases of *many* facts in this design but keep them separate from the *one* items they describe (they will eventually map to multiple tables in the database).

Step 3. If possible, review the existing documents (data entry forms, reports, etc.) that are currently part of the process you're attempting to model. What kinds of information are currently being (or will need to be) captured? What do the reports or printouts look like? What facts do they report? This is a critical step during database design since reports always contain information that will be required in your design.

If forms or reports do not yet exist, meet with the key players in this process and have them describe to you what they envision for data entry forms and data reports. Note that the key player may only be yourself!

Ensure that your design, as it appears in Step 2, satisfies the requirements of the current or proposed input forms and reports. Modify your design as necessary following your review of the required forms and reports.

Step 4. Create a list of the reports required, and from your investigation of the data input needs, you may also create a list of the various data entry forms required as well.

Step 5. Review your findings with the key players involved. Where appropriate, revise lists or repeat any of the steps above.

Step 6. Using your original (or revised) map from Step 2, draw out the relationship joins to connect the tables in the way you think best reflects the real world situation.

Example: A Typical Needs Assessment

We'll outline the major tasks associated with designing a database by way of a simple example. Along the way we'll introduce concepts such as *data types* and the process of *database normalization* and we'll end by discussing various *table joins*. Data types will be discussed in a bit more detail in the following chapter.

Imagine that you work for a non-governmental organization (NGO) that frequently sends staff on missions to other countries. You have been asked to build a database to track staff assignments on missions. An analysis of the current tracking effort reveals the following types of data are being collected and stored in an Excel worksheet:

- Staff Name, Staff ID, Department, Building, Office number, Office phone, Staff work skills, Staff mission assignments.

- Mission Country, Mission ID, Mission Start and End Dates, Mission Purpose, and Mission Staffing.

An analysis of the reporting requirements indicates that management needs reports for the following purposes:

- To determine staffing for every mission whether completed, in progress, or planned.

- To view workload for individual staff (the missions a staff member has been assigned).

Further, the current worksheet application uses two separate sheets for data entry: one for entering and tracking staff information and another for entering and tracking mission-related information.

The elements of this proposed database center around two unique sets of objects: **Staff** and **Missions**. Everything tracked by the current worksheet application relates directly to these two groups of objects.

A tentative sketch of the database map might appear similar to the following:

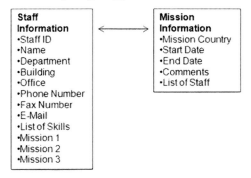

Task 2. Table Design

This phase of the design process involves converting the list of facts associated with your objects (in this example, Staff and Missions are each objects) into a table design. A database uses tables, which are made up of rows and columns.

- Each column in the table refers to a single *field*. Fields store only one type of fact. An example of a field is *Work Phone Number*.

- Each row in the table refers to a single *record*. Records store all the facts about the things, places, or events that your database models. All the facts concerning a particular staff member would appear on a single row.

Although the nature of fields is discussed more thoroughly in later chapters, you should know that part of designing a table and its associated fields is determining the type of data each field will store. We will use only a few of the available data types in our example but they will be discussed in greater detail in the following chapter.

Example: Proposed Table Designs

From the tentative map drawn up in the previous task example, two tables emerge:

Staff Information

Field Name	Data Type
Staff ID	Text
Staff Name	Text
Staff Department	Text
Building	Text
Office Number	Text
Phone Number	Text
Fax Number	Text
E-mail	Text
List of Skills	Memo
Mission 1	Text
Mission 2	Text
Mission 3	Text

Mission Information

Field Name	Data Type
Mission Country	Text
Start Date	Date/Time
End Date	Date/Time
Comments	Memo
List of Staff	Text

Task 3. Assign Primary Keys

A primary key is a field or a combination of fields in each table that ensure each record in a table:

- Describes a single entity, and
- Eliminates the possibility of duplicate rows (records).

Some tables contain fields that are easy to identify as candidates for a primary key. Other tables require an analysis of combinations of two or more fields. If your proposed table lacks a clear candidate, most database systems provide an *autonumber* or *auto increment* data type to create an artificial primary key.

Warning: Using an autonumber for a primary key will only prevent duplicate numbers in the primary key field. It is still possible to enter duplicate data into the table, unless you use one or more indices. Using an index to prevent duplicate data is discussed in Chapter 3.

It is not essential that all tables have primary keys, although you cannot relate tables using joins to model most relationships without using primary keys.

Developers frequently draw up a list of *candidate primary keys* to review the potential benefits and problems with each. Once a field or a combination of fields is selected they are then referred to as the *primary key field(s)*.

Example: Identifying the Primary Keys for the Proposed Tables

In the proposed **Staff Information** table, the most obvious choice is **Staff ID**, although there are other potential candidates (the combination of Staff name and Office number for example). In the proposed **Mission Information** table an analysis of *candidate primary keys* yields no single field.

- **Mission Country** is insufficient because there may be several missions to a particular country.
- **Start Date** is insufficient because several missions may start on the same date.

- **List of Staff** is insufficient because it may be possible for the same team to go on another mission.

Without a clear single field, a developer then considers combinations of fields.

- **Mission Country** *and* **Start Date** are good candidates as no two missions to the same country ever depart on the same date.

Thus the primary key for the **Staff Information** table is the **Staff ID** field while the combination of **Mission Country** and **Start Date** serve as the primary key for the **Mission Information** table.

 If it were possible that two missions to the same county *can* depart on the same date, then the proposed **Mission Country** and **Start Date** fields would not work as the primary key. A careful analysis would be required to find an additional field which, taken together, would serve as a primary key. This underscores the difficulty at times in assigning a good primary key to a table.

Task 4. Normalize the Tables

Normalization is a process used to ensure that your database will store data as compactly and efficiently as possible. It guarantees that when you need to retrieve information from the database, you know exactly which field stores that information.

There are many rules of normalization but most database developers find that adherence to the first three rules is sufficient for good design. Each of the three rules will be presented along with commentary regarding our proposed tables. Where appropriate, corrective design measures will be suggested.

First Normal Form (1NF): All fields in a table are atomic

This rule states that each field stores only one fact and no more. A corollary to this rule is that you should not have multiple fields that store the same type of facts in the same table.

Commentary on First Normal Form

This rule makes sense when you consider how a table that violates the rule will fail at several important database tasks. For example, consider the following:

- If the entire staff name (first, middle, and last) is stored in a single field, how do you sort staff by last name?

- If you need to know who has gone on a mission to Peru (and the table contains fields such as *Mission1, Mission2* and *Mission3)*, which field do you look in?

- What happens if a staff member goes on a fourth mission when the table only stores information for three missions? Do you add another field to the table just to handle one exception?

Example: Normalizing the Database to 1NF

Staff Information Table

- The **Staff Name** field actually stores up to three facts, **First Name**, **Middle Name**, and **Last Name**. Break out this field into three separate fields (otherwise how could you search by first or last name?)

- A similar situation in the same table is found with the **List of Skills** field. Storing a list of skills in a single field is asking for trouble. How do you easily search such a field to find all employees with *mediation* skills? Break the Skills into a separate table (it is really modeling a *one-to-many relationship* between Staff and their few or numerous skills).

- **Staff Information** also contains three fields that really store the same information, **Mission 1**, **Mission 2**, and **Mission 3**. In its current state, to search on staff who have been on a mission to Brazil you need to search three separate fields. As we've seen before – the real problem arises when a staff member goes on a 4th mission. The solution is the same as that used for **List of Skills**. Remove the mission list to another table. Note that the relationship between Staff and Missions is really *many-to-many* because one staff member may go on many missions and each mission may have many staff. We will hold this point and return to discussion of this type of relationship and its implementation on page 25.

Mission Information Table

- The problem with this table is its reference to the **List of Staff**. This is conceptually the same as the last problem discussed with the Staff Information table. This field should be moved to another table. For the time being, we will again note that this relationship is really a *many-to-many* relationship.

Second Normal Form (2NF): Every non-key field should be fully dependent on the primary key field(s)

The intent of this rule is to ensure that fields in a table only describe one thing or entity. The fields that are not part of the primary key must fully depend on the primary key to justify their inclusion in the table.

Commentary on Second Normal Form

This rule forces a closer inspection of proposed fields in a table. In a fully relational database, tables are configured to store facts about a thing, event, or place. For each field in a proposed table, the essential question to ask is, "is this fact fully dependent on the primary key? Or, would I have known about this fact independent of the primary key?"

Example: Normalizing the Database to 2NF

If we assume that our organization is set up so each department occupies only one building (and in some organizations this is an assumption you cannot make!) then the field **Building** in the table **Staff Information** violates Second Normal Form. We can deduce the **Building** value by noting the **Department** value. This deduction does not involve our primary key (**Staff ID**)!

The solution would be to move **Building** to another table. In this example, we will forget storing this fact altogether since by knowing the **Department** we can deduce the **Building** value.

Third Normal Form (3NF): All non-key fields must provide a fact about the key field

Our current proposed design lacks a clear violation of third normal form, but an example would be to include *CountryPresidentName* in the **Mission Information** table. It may appear to be related, since missions go to specific countries but it isn't. The primary key in this table is the combination of **Country** and **StartDate**, and the current president of the county being visited isn't directly related to those facts.

Another variation on a violation of third normal form is the inclusion of one or more fields that contain *calculated* values. If the **Staff Information** table contained the fields **Staff Base Salary**, **Staff Benefits** *and* **Staff Total Cost** (with this field being the sum of the other two), it would violate 3NF. The reason is that the **Staff Total Cost** field isn't completely dependent upon **StaffID**. Its dependency is on two other fields in the table.

Commentary on Third Normal Form

Violations of third normal form are rare in a well-designed database as designers typically have an inherent sense when a proposed field doesn't directly relate to the table's primary key. It is more common however to find calculated fields in proposed table designs.

In general, it isn't a good idea to define a field that relies on calculations based on other fields in the table because we can conduct such calculations as we need them in a query, on a form, or in a report. Storing calculated values raises two problems:

- How do you ensure that the value is correctly updated if someone changes a dependent value in another field? Remember that databases do not behave like spreadsheets. The cells in a database table are not connected to one another via formulas that automatically update.

- Why store facts that can be calculated? As a developer, you can add the capacity to calculate the required data through queries, forms, and reports. This is the preferred method of supplying users with such information and ensures that each time a report is printed the calculated data are correct.

Example: Normalizing the Database to 3NF

Our proposed tables do not have any violations of third normal form. If fields were present that depended upon some calculation based on other fields within the same table, or contained fields that obviously didn't directly relate to the primary key we'd be in violation. Removing the calculated field and/or fields which don't directly relate to the primary key would solve the issue.

Example: Result of Normalizing the Proposed Database Design

If each of the solutions indicated in the preceding sections were followed, the proposed design would appear as:

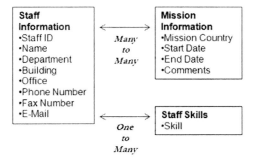

Interim Review of the Proposed Design

At this point, it would be a good idea to repeat Tasks 2, 3, and 4 on page 16 because new tables have been introduced to the proposed database design. After generating a new table and field list and a closely inspecting the new tables to ensure they have appropriate primary keys and have been normalized, you should proceed with Task 5.

Task 5: Construct Table Joins

The last major task of the database design process is to establish the various joins between the proposed tables. A join is made between tables by connecting one or more fields that the tables have in common. A join is used in a relational database as an instruction to the database system regarding how to relate records between tables.

One or more fields in each table may participate in the join. You achieve different join types depending on whether the selected fields constitute the primary key for each table. This interaction between a join and a table's primary key is outlined in the table below.

When the joined field from one table is a primary key but the joined field in the second table is not a primary key, the field in the second table is called a *foreign key*. Foreign keys are more a concept than an actual database component in that, unlike a primary key there is no requirement that a foreign key field be specifically noted as such when designing a table.

Types of Joins

Join	Implementation
One-to-one	A primary key field in one table is joined to a primary key field in a second table. This type of join is relatively rare and is used mainly for tables that store additional, rarely accessed facts.
One-to-many	A primary key field in one table is joined to a *non-primary key* field in a second table. The non-primary key is known as a *foreign key*. This is the most common join seen in a relational database.
Many-to-many	No relational database can model a many-to-many join between two tables. A third table, known as a *join* table or more commonly a *bridge* table, is used as an intermediary. The bridge table contains fields that match the primary key fields in the two other tables.
	A primary key field in one table is joined to a *non-primary key field* in the bridge table (this creates a *one-to-many* join). From the other table, a primary key field is also joined to a *non-primary key* field in the bridge table (this also creates a *one-to-many* join). It is helpful to think of a *many-to-many* join as two *one-to-many* joins involving three tables. Constructing this type of join is discussed beginning on Page 27.

This chapter is concerned about the theory of joining tables, not the practice. The step-by-step procedure for constructing joins is addressed on page 69.

Primary keys must be designated when you design a table. However, in Access, a *foreign key* is a concept and there is no special step required to designate one during table creation. The topic of assigning a primary key to a table is discussed on page 54.

Notes on Implementing a One-to-Many Join

One-to-many joins are fairly straightforward as long as you keep the following points in mind.

- The table on the *one* side of the join contains a field or fields that constitute the table's primary key. The primary key field is joined to a corresponding field in the table residing on the *many* side of the join.

- The joined field or fields on the *many* side may not constitute the table's primary key (although in conjunction with other fields in the table, they may be a part of that table's primary key).

- The field names need not match between tables, but the *data type* must match. Field data types have not yet been addressed. At this point, it is important to simply note that if one field in a join stores data such as date/time information, then the corresponding joined field in the other table must store the same type of information.

Example: Joining Two Tables in a One-to-Many Relationship

To join the proposed **Staff Information** table to the **Staff Skills** table the following conditions must first be met:

- The **Staff ID** field in the **Staff Information** table must be the table's primary key.

- A corresponding field in the **Staff Skills** table must exist and store the same type of information as **Staff ID** in the **Staff Information** table. This field must not be the primary key for table **Staff Skills**. For convenience, this new field will also be named **Staff ID**.

- It would be a good idea to establish a primary key in table **Staff Skills**. With only two fields, the primary key would be a combination of both **Staff ID** and **Staff Skill**. This does not violate the previous condition because the primary key in **Staff Skills** is not simply **Staff ID** but a *combination* of **Staff ID** and **Staff Skill** (and it serves the purpose of preventing duplicate skills for a given staff member).

The adjusted tables, their primary keys, and the one-to-many join would appear as:

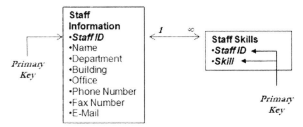

To visualize how a one-to-many join appears once the tables are populated with data, consider the following two tables (the primary keys are *Bold Italic*).

Table: Staff Information

Staff ID	First Name	Last Name	Department
A01	Barbara	Smith	Finance
A67	Enrico	Garcia	Management
B05	Noriko	Tawaska	Management
C44	John	King	Logistics

Table: Staff Skills

Staff	Skill
A01	Mediation
A01	Language translation
A67	Multilingual software support
B05	Mediation
B05	Project management
B05	Event planning

The following facts may be deduced from these tables and their implied relationship:

- No Staff ID values are duplicated in table **Staff Information** and no combination of Staff ID and Skill values are duplicated in **Staff Skills** as these fields constitute the primary keys for their respective tables.

- Barbara Smith is associated with two skills, Enrico Garcia with one, and Noriko Tawaska with three. John King has no skills listed in **Staff Skills**. This observation supports the fact that these tables are related in a *one-to-many* join.

- There are two staff members who have Mediation skills, Barbara Smith and Noriko Tawaska. This observation indicates that in a relational database, you can ask questions of the database starting from any side of a join.

Notes on Implementing a Many-to-Many Relationship

No relational database can model a many-to-many relationship using only two tables. A third table, the *join table* or *bridge table*, must be employed. This bridge table will contain the foreign keys from the other two tables.

It is easiest to think of the three tables as implementing two separate *one-to-many* joins (which is in fact what is done). You first consider the case from one table (the *one* side) to the bridge table (the *many* side) and then from the other table (the *one* side) to the bridge table (the *many* side).

The bridge table stores the facts that associate records between the other two tables. A bridge table that relates Missions and Staff would contain a record for each mission a staff member has been on. From the perspective of the mission table, the bridge table maintains a record for every staff assigned to any given mission.

Example: Joining Tables in a Many-to-Many Relationship

Joining the proposed **Staff Information** table to the **Mission Information** table requires a new bridge table, which will be named **Mission Members**. In order for the many-to-many join to work, the following conditions must be met:

- The **Staff ID** field in the **Staff Information** table must be the table's primary key.
- The **Country** *and* **Start Date** fields in the **Mission Information** table must be that table's primary key.
- The bridge table must contain foreign key fields to correspond to the primary keys of the other two tables. Thus, the new table will require a minimum of three new fields: **Staff ID**, **Country**, and **Start Date** (we are maintaining the same field names as exist in the parent tables but this isn't necessary. Ensuring that the data types are the same between each primary/foreign key link is required).
- A primary key in the bridge table consisting of all three fields would make a great primary key. Its task is to ensure that each staff member may only be associated once with a given country and mission start date.

The adjusted tables, their primary keys, the new bridge table (named **Mission Members**), and the one-to-many joins would appear as:

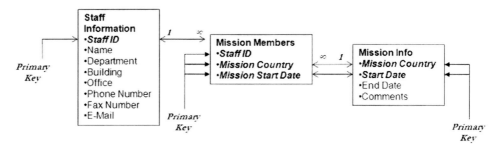

To visualize how a many-to-many join appears once the tables are populated with data, consider the following three tables (the primary keys are *Bold Italic*).

Table: Staff Information

Staff ID	First Name	Last Name	Department
A01	Barbara	Smith	Finance
A67	Enrico	Garcia	Management
B05	Noriko	Tawaska	Management
C44	John	King	Logistics

Table: Mission Members

Staff ID	Mission Country	Start Date
A67	Bolivia	04-Mar-2012
B05	Kenya	28-Jun-2012
C44	Bolivia	04-Mar-2012
C44	Bolivia	18-Jun-2012
C44	Turkey	15-Jun-2012

Table: Mission Information

Mission	Start Date	End Date	Comments
Bolivia	04-Mar-2012	19-Mar-2012	Final talks
Turkey	15-Jun-2012	20-Jun-2012	Consultation
Kenya	18-Jun-2012	28-Jun-2012	Final talks
Bolivia	18-Jun-2012		

The following facts may be deduced from these tables and their implied relationship:

- No staff member is duplicated in the **Staff Information** table (no violation of the table's primary key).

- No combination of **Mission Country** and **Start Date** values are duplicated in the **Mission Information** table (no violation of the table's primary key).

- No combination of **Staff ID, Mission Country**, and **Start Date** are duplicated in the **Mission Members** table (no violation of the table's primary key).

- Enrico Garcia and Noriko Tawaska have each been on one mission while John King has been on three. Barbara Smith has not been on a mission (you can ask questions from **Staff Information** to **Mission Information**).

- The staff who were on the mission to Bolivia that started on 04-Mar-2012 are Enrico Garcia and John King (you can ask questions from **Mission Information** to **Staff Information**).

Summary

Designing a database is as much art as technical science. The process is conceptually very similar to what architects go through when designing a building. We've outlined a few tasks which help provide a formal framework for the database design process. If you are attempting to encapsulate an existing process and/or set of facts reviewing the current process and the documents and reports associated with it will immeasurably help you in getting the design right. An obvious point is that reports contain summarization of the data (fields) your database will need and database developers rely heavily on such reports to ensure that the important fields are contained within the design.

Frequently the database developer will modify the proposed design and these changes may necessitate repeating some earlier steps to smooth out potential new issues. This is especially true when considering the first through third normal forms of a proposed design. Realizing that a proposed relation between two tables is actually a many-to-many relation will necessitate the addition of an intermediary bridge or join table.

Chapter 3 | Creating Tables

Tables are the core structure in any relational database design. It's often misunderstood that the term *relational* as it appears in the phrase *relational database* refers to the relations between tables (we referred to these as joins in the previous chapter). The word *relation* refers to the grid-like structure of tables within a database. The term is derived from a branch of mathematics and was formally described in 1970 by Edgar Codd who worked for IBM.

As previously discussed, a table consists of a regular grid structure. The columns denote *fields* which store specific facts about an object, location, or event while the rows resolve to individual *records* about that object, location, or event. As we've seen, related tables are denoted by defining joins, thus allowing one to create one-to-one, one-to-many and many-to-many relationships between the tables in a database.

One interesting point about relational databases is that the definition of each table within the database is also contained with a table structure. Tables really are the fundamental unit of organization in a relational database. In this chapter you'll learn how to create tables and work with many important table properties.

Creating a New Table

Now that the fundamentals of designing a database have been explored, we'll turn to the design of individual tables. In a database, a table is the fundamental unit of data storage. If you view the contents of a table it resolves as a grid made up of columns (fields) and rows (records). When designing a table, the design itself is displayed in a similar grid format of columns (field properties) and rows (fields). There are some differences between major database applications in how tables are employed but the general concept of a table being designed by using a table-like interface is a common feature of most database applications. Also common are many of the fundamental data types needed to define what kind of data will be stored in individual fields.).

Microsoft Access adds additional features to table design that may not be found in other database applications. The ability to create rules that validate data, masks that ensure that data fit a predefined scheme, built-in lookup fields to simplify and standardize some data entry are a few features we'll explore later in the discussion of table design.

Before creating a table, it is essential that you have completed your needs assessment. This includes working through all five tasks that are outlined beginning on page 15.

To create a new table, you should have:

1. A list of the fields that will make up the table.

2. A *data type* for each of the fields.

3. An idea of which field or fields will constitute the table's primary key (if required).

4. An idea of any field or combination of fields that may need to participate to enforce uniqueness among the records.

5. A list of the field or fields which should be *indexed* in order to speed up queries.

It is a good idea to use a primary key or a unique index for tables that will not participate in any relationships to other tables. Primary keys or unique indices ensure that records are not duplicated in the table.

Access 2010 includes a feature that allows you to add fields directly to a working table. This may be convenient but it's a very bad idea to add columns while working directly with data. It strongly suggests that not enough time went into the initial table design. We'll focus on the more formal approach to designing tables by using the table editor that has been included in all versions of Access.

In addition, some fields may have special data entry needs. The following table outlines additional points to consider for each of your fields. Note that as previously discussed, some of these attributes are specific to Microsoft Access and are not implemented in other database applications.

Special Field Properties

Property	Description
Formatting	You can control how data contained in a field is displayed. You may want to display dates in a specific format even though the database will permit users to enter dates in a variety of formats (unless an **input mask** has been applied).
Input Masks	If a field requires structured data, for example, for storing North American phone number or U.S. Social Security numbers, you can create an input mask that will enforce your structured data needs.
Validation Rules	If a field stores data that must adhere to a set of requirements, you can establish the requirements as rules. Data may not be stored in the field unless it satisfies the validation rule.
Required	For some fields (any that constitute the primary key) you may want to specify that data entry is required. For primary key fields this is set automatically to *true*.
Indexed	For fields that will be commonly used in queries and searches, setting an index will enhance the speed of the search. Note that fields that make up the primary key are automatically indexed.

How to Create a Table

Step 1.   Select the **Create** tab, and from the **Tables** group, choose **Table Design**. The **Table Designer** will appear similar to the following image.

The **Table Designer** consists of two horizontally-divided sections. The upper area is itself a table and is used to define the individual fields in your new table. There are three columns that accept entries for the field name, the data type, and any descriptive text you wish to enter. Each row will map to an individual field in your table.

The lower area, noted as **Field Properties** contains a list of all properties associated with the current field (in the image the first field, tentatively named ID is the current field). The associated properties will vary depending upon the field's data type. In the illustration the data type is *Autonumber* which as you can see in the properties area is actually a *long integer*. Long integers are whole numbers (no decimal or fractional parts) that can occur within the range -2,147,483,648 to 2,147,483,647.

To the right of the list of field properties is a small display area that will display short descriptive text for the current property.

Step 2.   Add at least one field to your table design (Access will not permit the creation of a table without fields.

Step 3.   Save your table design (procedure follows).

 If you create a new table by first choosing **Table** in the **Create** group (rather than choosing **Table Design**), Access automatically creates a primary key field named *ID* and sets the data type to *AutoNumber*. You can delete this field if necessary while in **Table Design View.**

Saving a Table Design

Once you have defined the table fields and have adjusted field properties, you should save the table design. Access will automatically prompt you to save a design if you attempt to move to Table Datasheet view or to close the Table Designer when changes have been made but not saved.

The **Save** command saves the design of the table. When you enter data into a table Access automatically saves the data. If you change the sort order, filter a table, or reorder columns and you attempt to close the table, Access may prompt you to save changes to the design of the table. Under these circumstances you may not wish to save such changes as the new sort order, filter, or reordered columns become part of the table design.

How to Save a Table Design

Step 1.   From the **Quick Access** toolbar, select **Save.**

Step 2.   In the **Save As** dialog box, enter a name for your table. If desired, refer to Appendix A for suggested naming conventions.

Step 3.   Choose **OK.**

Step 4.   If the table does not contain a primary key, the following message box will
           appear:

Step 5.   Choose **Yes** to let Access create an AutoNumber primary key or **No** to save the
           table without a primary key. Choose **Cancel** to return to the **Table Design**
           view in order to establish a primary key yourself.

Using an AutoNumber primary key is a common way to quickly assign a
field that can be used as a primary key and hence participate in table joins.
However, an AutoNumber does not ensure that the meaningful data in the
table is not duplicated. To ensure that the other data in your table can't be
duplicated between records, consider using an index to maintain uniqueness.
See page 51 for details.

Tables can be renamed, copied, deleted, or imported into another database.
Refer to Appendix A for discussion on naming and maintaining database
objects.

Table Design Tools

Table Design View gives you the most control over table creation. You create new fields and
adjust field properties using the **Table Tools | Design** tab and its associated groups, as well as by
using components of the **Table Design** view.

You display the **Table Design** tab by choosing **Table Tools | Design** from the ribbon area
when viewing a table in **Datasheet View**.

Components of the Table Tools | Design Tab

Group	Description
View	Alternates between table design and data views.
Tools	Contains tools for setting the primary key, building expressions, checking validation rules, and inserting and deleting rows.
Show/Hide	Toggles display of the table properties and indices sheets.
Field, Record and Table Events	Displays controls for attaching predefined macros to specific events in one or more fields in your table.
Relationships	Opens the **Relationship** or **Object Dependencies** windows.

How to Define a Table Field

See the note on Page 32 concerning the automatic creation of a primary key field when you create a new table. In this procedure we'll assume that we start with a table that has no primary key field automatically applied. If you intend on establishing a primary key for your table it is a good idea to establish the key in the first row of the table.

Step 1.   On the **Table Design** view, select the first blank cell in the **Field Name** column.

Step 2.   Type a field name (see the note below).

Step 3.   Choose an appropriate **Data Type**.

Step 4.   Although optional, type a **Description** for the new field.

Step 5.   Adjust any **Field Properties** for the new field. Field properties are discussed following Field Data Types, below.

Step 6.   To add additional fields, select the **Field Name** cell for the next blank row and repeat Steps 1 through 5.

 You must define at least one field before you can save the table design. Access will not permit you to save a blank table.

When naming a field, avoid abbreviations and name the field in a manner that clearly indicates the field's purpose. Although blank spaces in field names are permitted, some database systems do not accept blank spaces in field names. Spaces should be avoided if your database will eventually interact with another database or if you intend to eventually migrate your database to an database management system. To ensure future compatibility with other databases you may wish to adopt one of two space-less schemes: CamelCaseNaming simply combines two or more words with each word beginning in upper case. Under_Score_Naming replaces spaces with the underscore character.

Field Data Types

Part of the task of defining a field is choosing the appropriate data type. Data typing ensures that the field is optimally configured to store data. Access offers a wide range of data types to suit most needs.

There are important reasons for choosing an appropriate data type:

- The size of the overall database file is optimized when fields are appropriately configured to store data.

- Searches are faster as searching through numeric, text and, date/time data all require different approaches.

- Added functionality comes with some data types. For example, date manipulation functions are available for fields configured to store date/time information and currency symbol masks are automatically associated with the currency data type.

- The database will automatically enforce certain validation of data. For example, Access will not permit the value 1.3 to be entered into a field of the *integer* data type. Nor would it permit the value 30 February to be entered into a date/time field.

Access Data Types

Data Type	Type of Data	Examples and Notes
Text	Alphanumeric characters (up to 255)	Bolivia Staff Development Center 4500 Wisconsin Avenue
Memo	Alphanumeric characters (up to 64K)	Stores the equivalent of 9 single-spaced pages of text.
Number	Numeric data	45 8.0345×10^{45} -12.003400565
Date/Time	Chronological data	14-Jan-2000 1/14/00 January, 14 2000
Currency	Numeric data formatted as decimal currency	$ 450.09 $ 0.10 € 450.09
AutoNumber	Auto-incrementing, sequential numbers	Starts with 1 and sequentially increments for each new record. You cannot control the start number.
Yes/No	Data that exists in only two possible states.	True No -1
OLE Object	Complex data from other applications.	Excel worksheet, graphic image, sound clip, etc.
Hyperlink	Hyperlinks to Internet locations or local documents.	www.example.com
Attachment	Stores file attachments which can be edited or viewed.	A Word or Excel file (among other supported types).
Calculated	Stores the result of a predefined expression. Note that this field type violates 3NF as discussed on Page 21!	TotalCost = Price + SalesTax
Lookup Wizard	Any of the other types (except OLE Object) that are selected from an existing table.	Lookup a list of staff names, states or countries, etc.

 Autonumber, hyperlink, attachment, and calculated are not classic data types and do not necessarily have equivalent types in other database systems. Likewise, the Lookup Wizard simply creates a procedure to lookup data from a list or from another table.

About Field Properties

Each data type has additional field properties associated with it. Note that some of these properties are discussed in detail in the remainder of this chapter. In addition, there are multiple settings for the **Field Size** property when working with the **Number** data type (in other database applications each of these maps to separate data types). The tables that follow outline the field properties in general and the various settings for **Number** data types in particular.

The **General** tab of the **Field Properties** area appears similar to the following:

Field Properties

Property	Applies to	Description
Field size	Text, Number, AutoNumber	Adjusts the size of the field for optimal data storage. For **Text**, the range is 1-255 characters. See the following table for **Number** values.
Format	Text, Memo, Number, Date/Time, Currency, AutoNumber, Yes/No, Hyperlink	Controls the appearance of data. There are categories of built-in formats that include Date and Time, Number and Currency, Text and Memo, and Yes/No. You can also create custom formats.
Input mask	Text, Number, Date/Time, Currency	Enforces a specific format for data entry. There are built-in input masks for common data such as Social Security or North American telephone numbers, or you can create your own input mask.
Caption	Text, Memo, Number, Date/Time, Currency, AutoNumber, Yes/No, OLE Object, Hyperlink	Sets the label contents for the field when displayed in a form or on a report. (This value can always be overwritten when designing forms or reports.)
Default value	Text, Memo, Number, Date/Time, Currency, Yes/No, Hyperlink	Establishes a value that automatically appears in all new records.
Validation rule	Text, Memo, Number, Date/Time, Currency, Yes/No, Hyperlink	An *expression* that defines the acceptable conditions for data to be accepted into the field.
Validation text	Text, Memo, Number, Date/Time Currency, Yes/No, Hyperlink	Sets the text that appears in a message box if a validation rule has been violated. The **Validation Rule** property must be set for this property to take effect.

Field Properties

Property	Applies to	Description
Required	Text, Memo, Number, Date/Time, Currency, Yes/No, OLE Object, Hyperlink	Indicates that data must be entered in the field. This rule is enforced for all existing and new records and applies when data is imported or pasted into a table.
Allow zero length	Text, Memo, Number, Hyperlink	Permits the storage of " " as valid data. This property and the **Required** property control whether fields store **Null** and/or zero-length strings (see the following note).
Indexed	Text, Number, Date/Time, Currency, AutoNumber, Yes/No	Determines whether the field is indexed. For fields that you anticipate will be searched frequency, set this property to **Yes**.
Unicode compression	Text, Memo, Hyperlink	Controls how text from Western Languages is stored in the database. By default, the property is set to **Yes**.
IME Mode	Text, Memo, Hyperlink	Controls text display when the computer's localization settings indicate a language that requires special processing (mainly languages that do not read left-to-right).
Decimal places	Number	Establishes the number of significant digits for a number or currency.
New values	AutoNumber	Controls whether AutoNumbers increment or are random.

Some database developers use **Null** to indicate *"I don't know"* and zero-length strings, " ", to indicate *"data definitely missing."*

Field Sizes for the Number Data Type

Setting/Size	Description
Byte **(1 byte)**	Whole numbers ranging from 0 to 255 only.
Decimal **(12 bytes)**	Decimal values ranging from -10^{28} to $+10^{28}$.
Integer **(2 bytes)**	Whole numbers ranging from -32,768 to +32,768.
Long integer **(4 bytes)**	Whole numbers ranging from -12,147,483,648 to +12,147,483,648.
Single **(4 bytes)**	Decimal values ranging from -3.402823E38 to -1.401298E-45 for negative values and from 1.401298E-45 to 3.402823E38 for positive values.
Double **(8 bytes)**	Decimal values ranging from -1.79769313486231E308 to -4.94065645841247E-324 for negative values and from 1.79769313486231E308 to 4.94065645841247E-324 for positive values.
Replication ID **(16 bytes)**	Used to store Globally Unique Identifiers (GUIDs) which are used when replicating or synchronizing two databases.

Field Formatting

Formatting controls how the data contained in a field will appear. Unless an **Input Mask** has been applied, data may be entered in a variety of formats. Once entered, however, the data is reformatted to fit the requirements of the field's **Format** property.

For example, a field with the **Date/Time** data type may have its **Format** property set to **Long Date**. In this format, dates appear with the name of the week and the month fully spelled out. An example of a long date is *Saturday, 22 September 2012*. If this field does not have an **Input Mask** applied, then you could enter any variety of non-ambiguous dates, such as 22-Sep-2012 or Sept 22, 2012, and the contents of the field would be formatted to *Saturday, 22 September 2012*.

There are a number of predefined formats that may be applied to some data types. In addition, you can create custom formats for these data types as well.

Predefined Formats

Data Types	Defined Formats	Example
Number	General	1234.567
	Currency	$1234.57
	Euro	€1234.57
	Fixed	1234.56
	Standard	1,234.6
	Percent	1,234%
	Scientific	1.234E+03
Date/Time	General Date	01-Jan-2001 11:59 AM
	Long Date	Monday, 01 January 2001
	Medium Date	01-Jan-2001
	Short Date	01/01/2001
	Long Time	11:59:30 AM
	Medium Time	11:59 AM
	Short Time	11:59
Currency	Same as for Number	
AutoNumber	Same as for Number	
Yes/No	Yes/No	Yes
	True/False	True
	On/Off	On

Some of the formats that appear for the date settings above will vary depending on the date/time settings of the local computer.

To review the list of possible custom formats for Text, Memo, Hyperlink, Currency, Number, and Date/Time data types, place the insertion point into a format property field for the desired data type and press **F1**, then choose the most appropriate help topic.

For text fields an **Input Mask** may make more sense than working with the **Format** property. For example, choosing an input mask for North American telephone numbers will automatically add area code parenthesis and a dash between the telephone exchange and number. This is easier than attempting to create a custom format rule for phone numbers stored in a text field. Input masks are discussed in the following section.

How to Apply a Format to a Field

Step 1.   Activate the desired field by selecting its **Row indicator**.

Step 2.   In the **Field Properties** area, select the **General** tab.

Step 3.   Select the **Format** text box.

Step 4.   For any of the field data types listed in the previous table except text and memo, select a predefined format from the drop-down list, or use **F1** to start on-line help to review rules required for a custom format. Enter any custom formatting characters or symbols directly in the **Format** text box.

Input Masks

Input masks are the complement of a field's **Format** property. As the name suggests, an input mask enforces a pattern that must be followed during data entry. If you set both the **Input Mask** and the **Format** property for a field you completely control how data is both entered and displayed.

Take care when designing an input mask to ensure that you have considered all possible cases that apply to the data the field will store. If any data fails the criteria of the input mask it cannot be stored in the field unless you redefine or remove the mask. This is important because an input mask vigorously guards the form data must take in order to be entered into the field. A good example is a single staff member with a telephone number in the United Kingdom's National Telephone Numbering Plan format when all other phone numbers in the table are enforced using a North American phone number input mask. Because the format of the phone numbers are different between the two localities, the mask will prevent the number in the United Kingdom style from being entered.

Like the **Format** property, there are a number of built-in masks that may be applied or you can create your own. The built-in masks only apply to the text or date/time data types.

Predefined Input Masks

Mask Name	Example
Phone Number	(123) 555-1234
Social Security Number	123-45-5678
Zip Code	09876-1234
Extension	62315
Password	**********
Long Time	3:12:00 PM
Short Date	16-Aug-2012
Short Time	03:12
Medium Time	03:12 PM
Medium Date	16-Aug-12

How to Apply a Predefined Input Mask

Step 1.   Activate the desired field by selecting its **Row indicator**.

Step 2.   In the **Field Properties** area, select the **General** tab.

Step 3.   Select the **Input Mask** text box. An ellipsis (…) will appear to the right of the text box.

Step 4.   Select the ellipsis. The **Input Mask** wizard will start.

Step 5.   From the list of input masks, select an appropriate mask.

Step 6.   Choose **Next**.

Step 7.   From the **Placeholder Character** drop-down list, choose a placeholder.

Step 8.   Indicate whether the symbols associated with the mask (if any) should be stored with the data.

Step 9.   Choose **Finish**.

 The placeholder is used when a field containing an input mask is empty. The characters are replaced as you enter new data into the field.

Creating Custom Input Masks

In addition to working with the predefined masks discussed above, you can create any number of custom masks. Custom masks are commonly used in conjunction with text fields when you need to define how organization-related numbers (such as a purchase order or patient ID) will be entered.

An input mask takes three arguments in the form: *Mask*; *Literal Display*; *Placeholder*. Note that semicolons must separate the arguments. The following table defines the input mask the arguments.

Argument	Description
Mask	The actual input mask. Refer to the next section for details of customized masks.
Literal Display	Determines whether literal characters (such as the parentheses in an area code) are stored along with the data. Use **0** to store the literal characters and **1** to ignore them. This argument is optional. If left empty, the default is to store only the data and not the literal characters.
Placeholder	Indicates a character to use for a placeholder. This argument is optional and if left empty, no placeholder is used.

In the first argument of the input mask, you specify the special characters that define the mask. Use the following table as a guide.

Input Mask Special Characters

Character	Description
0	Digit from 0–9, entry required, + and - not allowed.
9	Digit or space, entry not required, + and - not allowed.
#	Digit or space, entry not required, spaces displayed as blanks while editing but removed when data is saved.
L	Letters A–Z, entry required.
?	Letters A–Z, entry not required.
A	Letter or digit, entry required.
a	Letter or digit, entry not required.
&	Any character or space, entry required.
C	Any character or space, entry not required.
.,:;-/	Decimal and thousands, date and time separators. Note that these symbols depend on the computer's international settings.
<	Forces all characters to lowercase.
>	Forces all characters to uppercase.
!	Causes the mask characters to appear from right to left, rather than from left to right, although data entry proceeds from left to right.
\	Indicates that the next character is to be considered as a literal. You use this when you need to use one of the special characters above – for example to include the letter A in an input mask you would enter \A, otherwise A is interpreted as explained above.

Custom Input Mask Examples

Example	Description
>LL;1;A	Displays **AA** as placeholders. Requires two letters to be entered and forces them to uppercase. This is a good mask for U.S. state postal codes.
0000"-OPM"-LLL?;0;@	Displays @@@@-OPM-@@@@ as placeholders. Requires four digits before -OPM- and requires three letters after. The fourth letter is optional. The literal value -OPM- is stored with the data.
LL0000;;#	Displays ###### as placeholder. Two required letters followed by four required digits. Note that the second argument is ignored.
"IS-"09-0009;0;0	Displays IS-00-0000 as placeholders. Requires at least one digit in the first group followed by at least three digits in the second group. This would permit room locations such as IS-5-4050 and IS-12-344 to be stored. The placeholder IS- is stored.

For more information on custom input masks, place the insertion point in an input mask text area and press *F1*. Choose the appropriate help subject (here TextBox.InputMask property).

How to Create a Custom Input Mask

Step 1. Activate the desired field by selecting its **Row indicator**.

Step 2. In the **Field Properties** area, select the **General** tab.

Step 3. Select the **Input Mask** text box.

Step 4. Type the **Mask** argument of the input mask (use the previous two tables as guides).

Step 5. Type a semicolon (;) and type a 0 if you want the literal characters of the mask to be saved with the data. Otherwise enter a 1 to ignore literal characters.

Step 6. Type a semicolon and enter a character to serve as the placeholder.

Note that Steps 5 and 6 are optional.

Validation Rules

In situations where data must fall within specified ranges or adhere to a set of criteria, you can apply validation rules to ensure that your data requirements are enforced. A validation rule is an *expression* that is evaluated by Access. The evaluation must resolve to either *True* or *False*. If false, Access prevents the data from being entered into the field. If a **Validation Text** property is also established, a false evaluation will also display a message box containing the contents of the **Validation Text** property. Validation rules may be entered manually into the **Validation Rule** area during table design, or for complex validation rules you may wish to use the **Expression Builder**.

If you use **Validation Rules**, then it is a good idea to include **Validation Text**. Use this text to explain to the user the acceptable range of conditions.

Regardless of the route you take to build an expression, you may need to consult on-line help to understand the syntax of various expressions and functions.

Validation Rule Examples

Example	Description
>= #01-Jan-1990# AND <= Date()	Accepts dates between the first of January 1990 and today's date. *Note that in Access, dates are delimited using the pound (#) sign.*
<> 0	The value cannot be zero.
Like *USDA*	The value must contain "*USDA*". The exact position of USDA is not specified. *Note that in Access, the asterisk (*) is used as a wildcard operator.*
Like "USDA*"	The value must contain USDA as the first four characters of the data.
<100 OR =>200	Numbers must be less than 99 or greater than or equal to 200.

How to Create a Validation Rule Using the Expression Builder

Step 1.   Activate the desired field by selecting its **Row indicator**.

Step 2.   In the **Field Properties** area, select the **General** tab.

Step 3.   Select the **Validation Rule** text box. An ellipsis (...) will appear to the right of the text box.

Step 4.   Select the ellipsis. The **Expression** Builder will start. A dialog box similar to the following will appear:

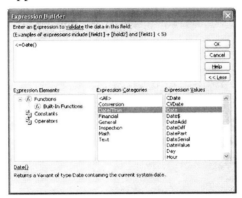

Components of the Expression Builder

Component	Description
Expression Box	Displays the expression as it is being built. You can directly enter text in this area or select **Operators** or items from the **Function List**.
Expression Elements	Lists the major categories of functions, constants and operators available.
Expression Categories	Displays major categories associated with the currently selected item in the **Expression Element** list.
Expression Values	Lists all functions contained within the category selected in the **Expression Categories** list. Double-clicking an item will insert it into the **Expression Box**.

Step 5.   If required, begin your expression by choosing the appropriate **Operator** from the **Operators** listed in the Expression Elements area (you can also manually enter these from the keyboard).

Step 6.   Select a major category from the **Expression Elements** list. Generally you will work with predefined functions.

Step 7.   Select a category from the **Expression Categories** list.

Step 8.   Select a function from the **Expression Values**. Double-click on the function to insert it into the **Expression Box**.

Step 9.   Continue with Steps 5 through 8 as required to continue building your expression.

Step 10.   Complete your expression and return to the **Table Design** view by choosing **OK**.

 You may need to edit the expression as it is being built. Some functions and operators will insert the text «Expr». This is a placeholder that indicates where you should enter expression text.

How to Manually Create a Validation Rule

Step 1.   Activate the desired field by selecting its **Row indicator**.

Step 2.   In the **Field Properties** area, select the **General** tab.

Step 3.   Select the **Validation Rule** text box.

Step 4.   Type your expression directly into the text box.

 If your expression is syntactically incorrect, an error message will appear when you attempt to move to another property text box or select another field. You'll need to correct any syntax errors before continuing.

How to Create Validation Rule Text

Step 1.   Select the desired field.

Step 2.   In the **Properties** area, select the **General** tab.

Step 3.   Select the **Validation Text** text box.

Step 4.   Type your validation text directly into the text box.

 To create a multiple line validation message, use the *Ctrl + Enter* key combination after your first line of text. Use the *right arrow* or *left arrow* keys to move between validation text lines.

Indexes

An index will greatly speed sorting, searching, and query operations that are directed against an indexed field. In all database applications there is a balance between the benefit of indexing and the number of indexed fields. Too many indices will affect the size of your database and may slow operations such as modifying existing records or inserting new records (both require re-indexing). Generally, you should index fields you think will commonly be acted upon for sorting and searching operations.

An index can also be used to enforce uniqueness among records. This is especially useful if you use an auto number field as the primary key in a table. In this case it would still be possible to duplicate records since the auto number field will never contain a duplicate.

How to Create an Index

This procedure is useful to create a single index based on a single field. For multiple indices, or to create an index based on two or more fields, use the procedure which follows.

Step 1.   Select the desired field.

Step 2.   In the **Field Properties** area, select the **General** tab.

Step 3.   Select the **Indexed** text box. A drop-down arrow will appear in the box.

Step 4.   Select the drop-down arrow. Choose the index option from the list of choices; as described below.

Option	Description
No	The field will not be indexed.
Yes (Duplicates OK)	An index will be built. Duplicate values between records are permitted.
Yes (No Duplicates)	An index will be built and duplicate values are not permitted. This setting is automatically applied if the field is a primary key.

How to Create Multiple Indexes

Step 1.   On the **Table Design** ribbon, select **Indexes**. A dialog box similar to the following will appear:

Step 2.   Enter a name for your index in the **Index Name** text box.

Step 3.   Select a field from the **Field Name** drop-down list.

Step 4.   Specify a sort order for the field.

Step 5.   Adjust **Index Propertie**s as required.

Step 6.   To add an additional field to the index, in the next row leave the **Index Name** field blank and select another **Field Name**, or to create another index, repeat Steps 2 through 5.

Step 7.   Close the **Indexes** window when done.

 In the illustration above, the index *PrimaryKey* was created automatically by Access when a primary key field was specified. A second index, named *Staff* has been manually created. It will index three fields: StaffID, StaffLastName and StaffFirstName, in that order.

How to Use an Index to Enforce Uniqueness Among Records

If you use an auto number as a primary key it's still possible to end up with duplicate records in your table. To prevent this, you can establish an index – based on one or more fields – that enforces uniqueness.

Step 1.   Identify the field or fields that need to maintain uniqueness in your table.

Step 2.   Open your table in **Table Design** view.

Step 3.   From the **Table Design | Tools** ribbon, choose **Indexes**.

Step 4.   If necessary, create either a single or multiple field index as discussed in the previous two procedures, otherwise select the desired index.

Step 5.   In the **Index Properties** area, set **Unique** to *Yes*.

Step 6.   Save the table design.

Additional Field Properties

Field properties other than *Input Mask*, *Validation Rule*, and *Indexed* are modified by selecting parameters from a list of choices that appears whenever the appropriate property text box is selected. These field properties include **Required, Allow Zero Length**, and **Unicode Compression**. The properties are explained in the section beginning on page 37.

How to Select Field Properties from a List of Options

Step 1.   Activate the desired field by selecting its **Row indicator**.

Step 2.   In the **Field Properties** area, select the **General** tab.

Step 3.   Locate the appropriate field property and select the corresponding text box. A drop-down arrow will appear in the text box. The selected field will appear similar to the following:

Step 4.   Select the drop-down arrow to expose the list of choices.

Step 5.   Select the appropriate choice from the list box.

    Continually double-clicking in the text box for a field property will cycle through the list of choices.

Primary Keys

A primary key may consist of one or more fields in a table. Setting a primary key will automatically adjust the field's **Indexed** property to **Yes (No Duplicates)**. When you work with multiple field primary keys, the **Indexed** property of each field will be set to **No**, but the **Unique** property of the fields will be set to **Yes** in the **Indexes** window. A table may contain only one primary key, although the key may be made up from multiple fields.

How to Set a Single Field Primary Key

Step 1.   Activate the desired field by selecting its **Row indicator**.

Step 2.   From the **Table Design** Ribbon, select **Primary Key**.

How to Remove a Single Field Primary Key

There are situations where you may need to remove a table's primary key. For example, encountering primary key violations (discussed beginning on Page 53) when attempting to import data may warrant temporarily removing the table's primary key.

Step 1.   Activate the desired field by selecting its **Row indicator**.

Step 2.   From the **Table Design** ribbon in the **Tools** area, select **Primary Key**. The **Primary Key** option for the desired field will be removed.

How to Set a Multiple Field Primary Key

Step 1.   Activate one of the desired fields by selecting its **Row indicator**.

Step 2.   If the other fields are adjacent to the first, hold down the *Shift* key and select the last field of the primary key, or if the other fields are not adjacent, hold down the *Ctrl* key and select each of the other fields of the primary key.

Step 3.   From the **Table Design** ribbon in the **Tools** area, select **Primary Key**.

How to Remove a Multiple Field Primary Key

Step 1.   Select any field that is part of the primary key.

Step 2.   From the **Table Design** ribbon in the **Tools** area, select **Primary Key**.

Troubleshooting Primary Keys

If you attempt to establish a primary key in a table that already contains data, you may encounter difficulty. In general there are two types of errors that may arise.

Duplicate Values in the Primary Key

This error message will appear if you try to establish a primary key on a single or multiple set of fields and there are duplicate field values among those fields.

To fix this problem, perform the following steps:

Step 1.   Remove the current primary key (this error arises when you try to save a table in **Table Design** view after you have established the primary key).

Step 2.   Close the **Table Datasheet** view.

Step 3.   Create a new query and choose the **Find Duplicates Query Wizard** (see page 96 for more information on creating queries).

Step 4.   Choose the table you were working with.

Step 5.   Choose the field or fields that are intended to be the table's primary key.

Step 6.   Choose **Finish** and run the query.

Step 7.   Note the duplicate values that appear in the **Query Datasheet** view. In the case of many duplicates, you may wish to print the view.

Step 8.   Open the table in **Table Datasheet** view and use **Find** or **Sort** or **Filter** operations to locate the records indicated by the query results in Step 7.

Step 9.   Remove duplicate records or change field values among the potential primary key fields to remove the redundancy.

Step 10.   Return to **Table Design** view and establish the primary key.

Index or Primary Key Cannot Contain a Null Value

This error message commonly occurs if you attempt to set a multiple-field primary key and one or more of the fields is blank. No single field value may be blank (or Null) in a primary key, and this rule also applies to those fields that are participating in a multiple-field primary key.

To fix this problem, perform the following steps:

Step 1.   Remove the current primary key (this error arises when you try to save a table in **Table Design** view after you have established the primary key).

Step 2.   Change to the **Table Datasheet** view.

Step 3.   Select the field you intend to serve as primary key. In the case of a multiple-field key, select the first field in the group.

Step 4.   From the **Home** Ribbon, in the **Sort & Filter** group, select **Sort Ascending.**

Step 5.   Correct any blank values in the field.

Step 6.   If you are attempting to establish a multiple-field primary key, select the next field and repeat Steps 4 and 5 until you have examined all fields and corrected any blank values.

Step 7.   Return to **Table Design** view and establish the primary key.

Lookup Fields

A lookup field uses a custom list, or field data from a table, to provide a list of choices when entering data into the field. Lookup lists are very useful in simplifying data entry and in preventing bad data entry (such as typographical errors or spelling mistakes). When you create a lookup list for a table, any query or form that is based on the table will inherit the lookup list. Examples of lookup lists include:

- A list of divisions, departments, or buildings for an organization.

- A list of States, Provinces, Regions, or Countries.

- A list of employees, arranged by last and then by first name (lists can display multiple fields although they may only provide a single value for storage into a field).

Although you can create a lookup list manually, working with the **Lookup Wizard** is far easier.

 As mentioned above, if you create a lookup field in a table, any form based on that table will inherit the lookup ability (using a combo box). You can also elect to create a lookup control on a form and not add this feature to the underlying table.

How to Create a Lookup Field that Uses a Custom List

Step 1.   If the current table design has not been saved, save it before proceeding.

Step 2.   Create a new field or select an existing field.

Step 3.   In the **Data Type** field, activate the drop-down list and choose **Lookup Wizard** from the options. The first dialog box of the **Lookup Wizard** will appear similar to the following:

Step 4.   In the first dialog box of the **Lookup Wizard**, choose **I will type in the values that I want** and choose **OK**. The second dialog box of the **Lookup Wizard** will appear similar to the following:

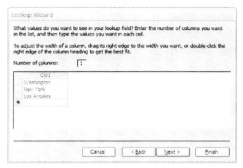

Step 5.   Indicate the number of columns the lookup field will contain. Note that only the contents of the first column will be stored in the field.

Step 6.   Type the values you wish to display in the column (or columns) indicated. Use the **Tab** or **down arrow** key to add additional items to the list. When finished typing your custom values, choose **Next**. The last dialog box of the **Lookup Wizard** will appear similar to the following:

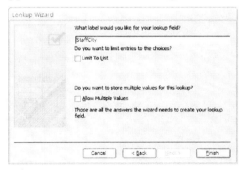

Step 7.   Provide a name for the column or accept the displayed value.

Step 8.   If you wish to limit data entry to the list you created, check the **Limit to List** checkbox. If unchecked, users can enter additional terms that are not contained within your list. If checked, data entry is restricted to items on your custom list.

Step 9.   Check **Allow Multiple Values** if you intend to let users store more than one item from your list. If checked, the drop down box will contain check boxes that permit users to choose among the items in the list (for example, by checking New York and Boston both values are stored).

Step 10.   Choose **Finish** when done.

How to Create a Lookup Field that Uses Existing Table Data

Many developers create *lookup tables* specifically for this purpose. For example, a table that lists the departments in a major organization would serve to feed the *Department* lookup field in a staff table. If a new department is created its name is entered in the lookup table and immediately becomes available to any lookup fields based on that table. As previously mentioned, lookup fields used this way prevent typographical and spelling errors when conducting data entry. This ensures that future queries and grouped reports return data correctly.

Step 1.   If the current table design has not been saved, save it before proceeding.

Step 2.   Create a new field or select an existing field.

Step 3.   In the **Data Type** field, activate the drop-down list and choose **Lookup Wizard** from the options. The first dialog of the **Lookup Wizard** will appear similar to the following:

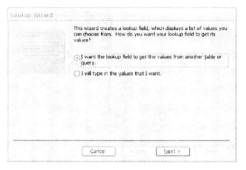

Step 4.   In the first dialog box of the **Lookup Wizard**, choose **I want the lookup column to lookup the values in a table or query** and choose **OK.** The second dialog box of the **Lookup Wizard** will appear similar to the following:

Step 5.   In the **View** area, choose the class of objects to list and select the target table or query.

Step 6.   Choose **Next**. The third dialog box of the **Lookup Wizard** will appear similar to the following:

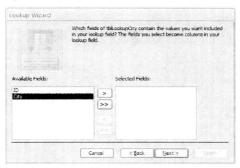

Step 7.   In the list of **Available Fields**, move the desired field into the **Selected Fields** area by selecting the field and then selecting the **Add (>)** button (you can also double-click on the field).

Step 8.   To add additional fields, continue Step 7.

Step 9.   Choose **Next** when the desired fields have been added. The fourth dialog box of the **Lookup Wizard** will appear similar to the following:

Step 10.   If desired, choose the field or fields you wish to sort. The **Ascending** buttons are toggles and alternatively selecting them will permit you to choose **Descending** as well. Choose **Next** when ready. The fifth dialog box of the **Lookup Wizard** will appear similar to the following:

Step 11.   If you have selected a primary key field (or if the wizard has sensed the presence of this field), the **Hide key column** checkbox will appear. Unless you specifically wish for this column to be visible, it is recommended that you leave this option checked.

Step 12.   Adjust the width of the field or fields in your lookup and choose **Next**. The final dialog box of the **Lookup Wizard** will appear similar to the following:

Step 13.   Provide a name for the column or accept the displayed value.

Step 14.   Decide whether to enforce Data Integrity. If enforced, the values in your table may only match values from the lookup table. Further, if you choose to **Restrict Delete**, values from the lookup table *may not* be deleted if there are related records in your main table. Choosing **Cascasde Delete** has the opposite effect. Deleting a record from your lookup table *will also delete any related records* in your main table!

Step 15.   Check **Allow Multiple Values** if you intend to let users store more than one item from your list. If checked, the drop down box will contain check boxes that permit users to choose among the items in the list (for example, by checking New York and Boston both values are stored).

Step 16.   Choose **Finish**.

 Access may prompt you to save the table before completing the wizard. This is necessary since linking tables may create a new relationship. If prompted, it is alright to save the table.

How to Remove a Lookup Field

You can restore a field to a standard appearance by removing the lookup function.

Step 1.   In **Table Design** view, select the desired field.

Step 2.   Select the **Lookup** tab from the **Properties** area.

Step 3.   In the **Display Control** text box, choose **Text Box**.

Step 4.   Save your change to the table design.

How to Use a Lookup Field

If you create a lookup field for a table, you can use the lookup feature when working with the table in **Table Datasheet** view, or when working with a query or a form that is based on the table.

Step 1.   Select the lookup field.

Step 2.   Begin typing a field value. If the value is contained within the lookup list, an *Autofill* function will complete your typing, or, select the drop-down list and choose the appropriate value.

Note: if you created a lookup list that supports multiple values, the drop down box would appear similar to the following:

Modifying Table Design

You can add or remove fields from a table at any time. Inserting a new field has no implications regarding any existing data in the table. However, removing a field that contains data will irretrievably remove the data. If you attempt to modify or remove a field that is part of a relationship (joined to one or more other tables), you must delete the relationship join first (see Page 76 for details).

How to Select a Field

Step 1.   Position the cursor to the immediate left of the **Field Name** column. The mouse pointer will change to a right-pointing dark arrow (see illustration below.

Step 2.   Click to select the field.

How to Insert a New Field

You can insert new fields between existing fields in the **Table Design** view.

Step 1.   Select the field *below* the point where you wish to insert a new field.

Step 2.   From the **Table Design** Ribbon, in the **Tools** group, select **Insert Rows.**

 Selecting more than one row before using the **Insert Row** command will insert as many rows as are currently selected. The new rows will be inserted *above* the selected rows.

How to Delete an Existing Field

Step 1.   Select the field to remove.

Step 2.   From the **Table Design** Ribbon, in the **Tools** group, select **Remove Rows**, or press the *Delete* key.

Selecting more than one row before deleting will remove all selected rows.

Warning: If the deleted row is a field that contains data in the table, the data will be lost. Access will warn you of this condition. There is no undo function to restore the removed field and its data.

If you attempt to delete the field or fields that make up a table's primary key *and* the table is joined to other tables, then you must first remove the relationship join using the **Relationships** window. Once the join is removed, you can return to the **Table Design** view to remove the field or fields that make up the primary key.

How to Modify a Lookup Field

Step 1.   Select the desired field.

Step 2.   From the **Table Design** ribbon, **Tools** ribbon, choose **Modify Lookups**.

Step 3   The **Lookup Wizard** will start. Follow the directions beginning on Page 55 (for a custom lookup list) or Page 57 (for a lookup that uses data from another table).

How to Change Field Order

When you view a table in **Datasheet View** the order of the columns (left to right) is based on the order of the fields (top to bottom) as defined in **Table Design View**. If you reorder fields in **Table Design View** the new order is reflected in **Datasheet View**. Note however that if you reorder columns in **Datasheet View** and save the design, the order is saved only for **Datasheet View**. In this case the original column order is retained in **Table Design View**.

Step 1.   In **Table Design View**, select the column you wish to move.

Step 2.   Position the mouse over the **Row Selector** area (it should appear as a standard mouse-pointer with an upward-left pointing arrow).

Step 3.   Left-click and hold the mouse button while dragging the column to a new location.

Step 4.   Release the mouse when done.

 If you select multiple fields in Step 2 you can reorder a group of fields at the same time.

Chapter 4 | Joins

If tables are the fundamental unit of a relational database, the joins may be thought of as the glue that binds tables together. If a database only uses a single table, or it maintains two or more tables that are not related then joins are not necessary. For databases that need to model one-to-one, one-to-many and/or many-to-many relations then joins are essential components of the design.

Microsoft Access provides a specific set of tools to graphically create and manage joins. A similar tool will be available when you create and manage queries as well, and in fact you'll soon see that modifying join types when creating a query is a useful activity.

Relationships Window

Once tables have been designed, primary keys established, and foreign keys identified in the appropriate tables, individual relationship joins may be defined between tables. All aspects of relationship joins between tables in the database are manipulated through the **Relationships Window**.

The power of relationship joins in Access is twofold. First, you are able to fully realize the potential of relational database design as discussed in Chapter 2. Second, once relationship joins have been defined, Access remembers the relationships and makes creating complex queries, forms and reports (especially via the form and report wizards) much easier.

 You cannot create or modify relationship joins for a table that is opened in **Design View**. Ensure that all table design views are closed before working with the **Relationships Window**.

How to Open the Relationships Window

Step 1.   From the **Table Design** ribbon, **Relationships** group, select **Relationships,** or from the **Database Tools** ribbon, **Relationships** group, select **Relationships**.

Step 2.   If there are no relationship joins, the **Show Table** dialog box will appear similar to the illustration below. If one or more relationship joins have been established, the **Relationships Window** will open. This would mark the end of this procedure.

Step 3.   If the **Show Table** dialog box has opened, select a table to add to the **Relationships Window** and choose **Add**. Continue this step until the desired tables (or queries) have been added to the **Relationships Window**.

Step 4.   When all desired tabled (or queries) have been added close the **Show Tables** dialog box. The **Relationships Window** will appear similar to the following:

 Tables are represented as small windows that list the field names. Primary key fields are indicated with a key icon. Since foreign keys are a concept, they are not specifically identified in this type of view.

How to Add Additional Tables to the Relationship Window

Once you've added several tables to the **Relationships Window** you may find it necessary to add additional tables. If not already opened, open the **Relationships Window** and follow this procedure.

Step 1.	On the **Relationship Tools** ribbon, in the **Relationships** group, select **Show Table**.
Step 2.	Select a table or query from the list of tables or queries.
Step 3.	Choose the **Add** button.
Step 4.	Continue adding tables or queries as needed
Step 5.	Close the **Show Tables** dialog box when finished.

Creating a Relationship Join

The process of creating relationships between tables requires two steps:

- Indicating which fields between two tables are to be joined.

- Specifying properties of the join, including whether you wish to enforce **Referential Integrity**.

Referential integrity is a property that ensures that joined tables always remain synchronized. If you establish referential integrity *and* set **cascade update related fields**, then you can make changes to a table's primary key field and the database will automatically update the foreign key field in all related tables. If you also establish **cascade delete related** records, then deleting a record on the *one* side of a join will automatically remove all related records in joined tables. Referential integrity is discussed in more detail beginning on Page 73.

Dragging a join line between tables creates relationship joins. Depending on the presence or absence of primary keys in each table, Access will automatically assign the relationship type using the following rules:

Join Type	Rule
One-to-Many	One of the joined fields is a primary key in one table only.
One-to-One	The joined fields in both tables are the primary key.
Indeterminate	The joined fields in neither table are the primary key. This type of relationship should be avoided because you cannot establish referential integrity. There are some queries however where an indeterminate join is acceptable.

How to Create a Relationship Join (One-to-One or One-to-Many)

| Step 1. | If you have not already added the required tables to the **Relationship** window, follow the steps on page 65 to add additional tables. |

Step 2.   Start with the table that represents the *one* side of the relationship join. Position the cursor over the primary key field or one of the fields which makes up a compound primary key.

Step 3.   Click and drag the mouse over to the second table, position it over the foreign key (or the primary key if creating a one-to-one join), and then release the mouse. A dialog box similar to the following will appear:

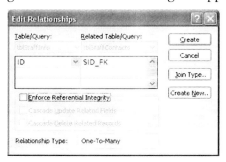

Edit Relationships Dialog Box

Option	Description
Table/Query	The upper drop-down list displays the table containing the primary key field. The lower drop-down list displays the primary key in that table, although all fields are contained within the list.
Related Table/Query	The upper drop-down list contains the table that either contains the foreign key, or in the case of a one-to-one join, the other table with a primary key. The field grid when activated will display a drop-down list that lists all the fields in that table. In a one-to-many join, the foreign key field will be displayed. In a one-to-one join, the primary key is displayed.
Enforce Referential Integrity	Checking this box enables referential integrity. It is highly recommended that you enable this feature.
Cascade Update Related Fields	When checked, editing the primary key field in one table will automatically cascade the edit to any other related table. It is highly recommended that you enable this feature. (This feature is discussed in more detail on page 73.)
Cascade Delete Related Fields	When checked, deleting a record from the table containing the primary key field will automatically cascade the delete and remove any other related records in all joined tables. It is highly recommended that you enable this feature. Note that deleting a record from a table containing the foreign key (the *many* side of the join) *does not* cascade the delete over to the primary key table. (This feature is discussed in more detail on page 73.)
Relationship Type	Displays the type of relationship join being defined. It is useful to verify that the join type you desire is indicated here. Refer to the troubleshooting section on page 74 if needed.
Join Type	Controls the manner in which queries can collect data from tables connected by a join. This is discussed on page 70.
Create New	Permits the creation of another join independent of the join you are currently defining.

Step 4. Review the table and field information as displayed to ensure that the correct primary and foreign key fields (or primary key fields in the case of a one-to-one join) are displayed. In the event that the field information is incorrect, use the field list drop-down lists to select the correct field.

Step 5. If you wish to enable referential integrity (highly recommended), check the **Enforce Referential Integrity** checkbox.

Step 6. If you wish to enable cascade updates (highly recommended), check the **Cascade Update Related Fields** checkbox.

Step 7.   If you wish to enable cascade deletions (highly recommended), check the **Cascade Delete Related Fields** checkbox.

Step 8.   If you wish to modify the join type (not recommended), choose **Join Type**. In the **Join Type** dialog box, change the join and return to the **Edit Relationship** dialog box.

Step 9.   Choose **Create** to establish the relational join. A typical one-to-many join in the **Relationships** window will appear similar to the following:

Let's take a moment and recap some discussion from Chapter 2 in the context of the image above. In this example there are two tables which are now modeling a one-to-many relationship: one containing staff information (tblStaffInfo) which will contain one row for each staff in an organization. The primary key in this table is the field named **ID**. The second table contains the zero to many skills associated with each staff member. The primary key in this table is the field labeled **SSID** and more importantly, the *foreign key* to the tblStaffInfo table is the field named **SID_FK**. As previously discussed, the primary and foreign key fields need not have the same names but they *must* be of the same data type (in this case both fields are numeric).

How to Create a Relationship Join (Many-to-Many)

All databases model many-to-many joins using three tables. Recall from the discussion beginning on page 25 that the third table, sometimes referred to as a *bridge* table manages two separate one-to-many joins.

Step 1.   Ensure that the two primary key tables and the bridge table have been added to the **Relationships Window**.

Step 2.   Drag a join line from the primary key of one of the tables to the corresponding foreign key in the bridge table.

Step 3.   Adjust the relationship join properties to ensure that the join is a one-to-many. It is also recommended that you enable enforcement of referential integrity.

Step 4.   Return to the **Relationships Window** and drag a join line from the primary key of the *other* table to the corresponding foreign key in the bridge table.

Step 5.   Repeat Step 3 adjusting the properties for the second join. A typical many-to-many join in the **Relationships Window** will appear similar to the following:

Again, let's recap the discussion of many-to-many joins from Chapter 2. In this example we're creating a many-to-many join between staff (tblStaffInfo) and projects (tblProjects). The idea being that a staff member can be assigned to zero or more projects and a project can have zero or more staff assigned to it. The bridge table in this case is tblStaffandProjects. It contains two foreign keys – SID_FK is the foreign key to the ID primary key in tblStaffInfo and PID_FK is the foreign key to the PID primary key in tblProjects. Each foreign key is part of a one-to-many relationship with one of the two main tables. In this example, the pair of foreign keys in the tblStaffandProjects table *together* make the primary key for that table. If you think about it this makes sense as a good pair for a primary key. The pair enforces the common-sense condition that no staff can be assigned more than once to a particular project (or no project should have any given staff assigned to it more than once). Bridge tables are interesting because they can model information *about* the linkage between the two main tables. In this case our bridge models the actual staffing of projects. In its purest sense we really only need foreign keys to the primary key in tblStaffInfo (SID_FK to ID) and the foreign key for the primary key in tblProjects (PID_FK – PID). Since each row records the fact that a particular staff has been assigned to a particular project we can use the bridge table to record additional facts about that assignment. In this case the bridge table contains two fields: ProjectAssignDate and ProjectAssignNotes that contain facts specific to the staff:project assignment event. In this case, when a staff member was assigned to a particular project and any notes about the assignment are also stored in the bridge table.

Join Types

There are three types of joins that Access can create when linking tables. In a newly created database with referential integrity enforced, you should not worry about adjusting the join type. If you are working with an existing database that did not enforce referential integrity, or you are importing data into tables from another data source, you may need to adjust the join type to analyze the database table contents.

Join types directly affect the results of queries. Note that it is preferable to alter the join type when designing the query, not when creating the relational joins. The joins in a query affect only the query, not the tables, whereas altering the join type between tables affects the tables and all queries based on those tables.

To understand join types, consider the following two related tables. Note that these tables violate referential integrity as the foreign key table contains records that have no match in the primary key table (for example, no one is associated with the skill *Project Planning*). Altering join types is mainly used in cases such as these to highlight potential problems in establishing referential integrity in an existing collection of data.

Table: Staff Information	
Staff (PK)	Office
Mary	CB 200
John	CB210
Tonya	CB 355

Tables Joined
One to Many

1→M

Table: Staff Skills	
Staff (FK)	Skill
Mary	Scheduling
Mary	Interpretation
Tonya	Mediation
Tonya	Facilitation
Tonya	Scheduling
	Project Planning

PK: *Primary Key*
FK: *Foreign Key*

Listed below are the results of a query that include the **Staff** and **Office** fields from **Staff Information** (the one side of the join) and the **Skill** field from **Staff Skills** (the many side of the join) when the join type is modified.

Equi-Joins

In an equi-join, only records that have matches between the primary and foreign key fields in both tables are displayed. This is the default join type across all types of relational databases, including Microsoft Access. The results of a query based on an equi-join would appear as:

Staff	Office	Skill
Mary	CB 200	Scheduling
Mary	CB 200	Interpretation
Tonya	CB 355	Mediation
Tonya	CB 355	Facilitation
Tonya	CB 355	Scheduling

Note that John is not listed in the query result because he does not have a corresponding record or records in the **Staff Skills** table.

Left Join

In a left join, *all* records from the *one* side of the join and only those records from the *many* side that have matching values in the joined fields are included in the results. The result of a query based on a left join would appear as:

Staff	Office	Skill
Mary	CB 200	Scheduling
Mary	CB 200	Interpretation
Tonya	CB 355	Mediation
Tonya	CB 355	Facilitation
Tonya	CB 355	Scheduling
John	CB 210	

Note that John's record is now displayed, although no skills are listed. You would use this type of join when producing a staff directory where you want to list everyone in the **Staff Information** table regardless of whether they have corresponding records in the **Staff Skills** table. Although as previously discussed you would define this join type in a query based on the two tables and not in the Relationships Window.

Right Join

In a right join, *all* records from the *many* side of the join and only those records from the *one* side that have matching values in the joined fields are included in the results. The result of a query based on a left-outer join would appear as:

Staff	Office	Skill
Mary	CB 200	Scheduling
Mary	CB 200	Interpretation
Tonya	CB 355	Mediation
Tonya	CB 355	Facilitation
Tonya	CB 355	Scheduling
		Project Planning

These query results indicate the presence of a skill, *Project Planning*, which is not associated with any staff. This is called *orphaned data* and violates referential integrity. A right join query such as this would identify those records in the foreign key table that must be removed before establishing referential integrity.

Referential Integrity

Referential Integrity is a concept in relational database design and management that ensures that the data in any foreign key field in a joined table all match data in the joined primary table. This ensures that data from the *many* side of a one to may join actually matches data in the table on the *one* side of the join.

Let's revisit the illustration from the earlier discussion of Join Types on page 70:

Table: Staff Information		Tables Joined	Table: Staff Skills	
Staff (PK)	Office	One to Many	Staff (FK)	Skill
Mary	CB 200	1→M	Mary	Scheduling
John	CB210		Mary	Interpretation
Tonya	CB 355		Tonya	Mediation
			Tonya	Facilitation
			Tonya	Scheduling
				Project Planning

PK: *Primary Key*
FK: *Foreign Key*

In this example, referential integrity is violated in the **Staff Skills** table. The skill *Project Planning* is not related to any staff in the **Staff Information** table. Such data are said to be *orphaned*. If these tables were imported into Access from another source and left in their current state, Access would prevent you from creating a one-to-many join and enforcing referential integrity (how to fix this is discussed in the next section). If you created these tables in Access and established a join with referential integrity enforced, Access would prevent you from entering a skill in the **Staff Skills** table that didn't specifically relate to staff member in **Staff Information**.

Cascading Actions and Referential Integrity

When referential integrity is enforced you can further specify how Access behaves when either the primary key field on the *one* side of a join is changed or how Access behaves when a record in a table on the *one* side of a join is deleted.

Cascade Update Related Fields causes Access to automatically update all foreign key values when their related primary key value is edited. For example, if a Staff ID value must be edited and it is the primary key in a **Staff** table, then cascade update will update any foreign key value in any related table automatically. If referential integrity and cascade update were not enforced, changing the Staff ID value in one table would orphan all related data in any joined table. If referential integrity is enforced and cascade update isn't, Access will prevent you from changing the value in any primary key field if there are related records in any joined tables.

Cascade Delete Related Fields allows you to delete a record in a table on the *one* side of a join and all related records in all joined tables will be deleted as well. If this option isn't enforced then Access will prevent you from deleting a record on the *one* side when records on the *many* side exist and are related. Again, if Access didn't enforce this rule, deleting a staff member from the **Staff** table would result in orphaned data in any related table, such as **Staff Skills**. If referential integrity is enforced and cascade delete isn't, Access will prevent you from deleting a record in a table on the *one* side of a join if there are related records in any other joined table.

Troubleshooting Joins

There may be situations where your join type does not match your expectations or Access prevents you from establishing a join. The former condition typically arises when you have forgotten to establish the correct primary and foreign keys. The latter condition arises commonly when table data already exists and the data violates referential integrity.

Join Type is Incorrect

- If you are attempting to establish a one-to-many or a one-to-one join and you create an indeterminate join instead, ensure that you are joining the primary and foreign keys between the tables (to create a one-to-many), or that you are joining the primary keys between the two tables (to create a one-to-one).

- If the join line lacks the small **1-1** or **1-∞** symbols, it is because you did not enable **Enforce Referential Integrity**.

Join Cannot be Created Because it Violates Referential Integrity

This situation arises when attempting to join tables that contain data that violates referential integrity rules. Generally it is because there is orphaned data in the table on the many side of a join, or in the case of a one-to-one join, one table contains records not matched in the other table.

The solution is to construct a query that joins the two tables and to modify the join property in the query to view the orphaned records (refer to join types section on page 70). Remember to include at a minimum the primary and foreign key fields from the tables.

- For referential integrity errors in one-to-many joins, set the query's join to right join. The orphaned records will show up in the table on the many side of the join. Either remove those records or edit them so they are matched by records in the table on the one side of the join.

- When working with a one-to-one join, you may need to run the query twice, first setting a left join and then a right join. This is required because you cannot know ahead of time which table contains the orphaned data.

 You can also run the **Find Unmatched Query Wizard** to locate the unmatched records.

Modifying Relationship Joins

Unless you are troubleshooting data imported from another source, or you've made a mistake in a table design and need to fix an incorrect join once the design of the table or tables has been modified, modifying a relationship join using the **Relationships Window** should be a rarely-conducted task.

That said, this is the same procedure you would use to modify the join between tables when designing a query and as discussed previously there are valid reasons to modify a query table join.

How to Modify an Existing Relationship Join

Step 1.   In the **Relationships Window**, locate the desired join and double-click on it.

Step 2.   From the **Edit Relationship** dialog box, choose **Join Type**. The **Join Properties** dialog box will appear similar to the following. Note that the specific text in the three options will vary depending upon the actual table names involved in the join.

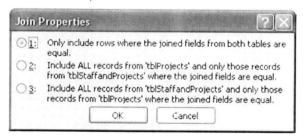

Step 3.   Select the desired join option. Option 1 creates an **Equi-Join**, option 2 creates a **Left Join** while option 3 creates a **Right Join**.

Step 4.   Choose **OK.**

How to Delete an Existing Relationship Join

Step 1.   In the **Relationships** window, locate the desired join and single-click on it.

 The join line should become slightly thicker when selected.

Step 2.   Press the *Delete* key.

 Data is not lost when a relationship join is deleted. However, if data entry occurs in either table, you may violate referential integrity rules and therefore make it difficult to reestablish the join at a later time.

How to Remove a Table from the Relationships Window

Step 1.   Select the desired table by clicking once anywhere on the table representation.

Step 2.   Press *Delete*.

 The table *is not* deleted from the database. It is simply removed from the **Relationships** window. Any joins between the removed table and the other tables are removed also.

Printing Relationships

You can create a printed copy of the **Relationships Window**. This is helpful when documenting your database design.

How to Print Relationships

Step 1.   Open the **Relationships Window**.

Step 2.   From the **Relationships Tools/Design** ribbon, in the **Tools** group, select **Relationship Report.**

The relationships will appear as a report opened in **Print Preview** view.

Step 3.　　If you need to change page orientation, use the page orientation controls located in the **Page Layout** group on the **Print Preview** ribbon.

Chapter 5 | Populating Tables with Data

In this chapter we'll discuss how to manually enter data into your database tables as well as the more common scenario of importing data from another source. As previously discussed many people begin management of data using a spreadsheet, which we now understand to be a bad approach. Since this is a fairly common scenario we'll focus on importing data from Microsoft Excel – it's relatively easy but there are limitations and the cleaner one can make the data in Microsoft Excel the easier importation becomes. Some of these same techniques will also help you in the event you need to import data from text files or from an existing relational database management system such as Microsoft SQL Server, MySQL, or Oracle.

Overview on Populating Tables

There are two broad methods you can choose from to populate tables with data.

- Entering data manually. This approach is generally used when the database is new and the information it will store has not yet been electronically manipulated.

- Importing existing data. Use this method if the data that the database will store has already been entered into a computer application. You can import from a variety of sources. Note that importing data may raise a number of issues involving primary key violations, referential integrity violations, validation rule errors, and input mask errors.

Points on Populating Tables

- In tables related by relational joins, the table on the *one* side of the join must be populated before the table on the *many* side. Another way of thinking about this is that the primary key field must first be established before a foreign key field can refer to it. Thus, especially when importing data, remember to import data into all the tables on the *one* side of a join before importing to the other related tables.

- Importing may cause problems if data coming into a table on the *one* side of a relational join has duplicate or null values in the primary key fields. Further, if data imported into the foreign key field of a table on the *many* side of a join lacks a counterpart in the primary key field of the table on the *one* side, a referential integrity violation error will occur.

- Validation rules and input masks will prevent the entry of data that violates the rule or the format of the mask. When manually entering data, you should correct the value before proceeding. When importing data, however, these field properties may prevent data from being imported at all. You may need to remove validation rules and input masks temporarily when importing data.

 Potential solutions to problems that arise during importation of data are discussed on page 91.

Entering Data into a Datasheet or Form

A table's **Datasheet** view presents the table data in a row and column format, making data entry simple and easy to read. The last row in a Datasheet is a blank record for adding a new record. The blank record is designated by the new record symbol, an asterisk (*).

A form's **Form** view presents the data in an arranged format, making data entry simple using text boxes, radio buttons, toggle buttons, check boxes, or drop-down lists. You step between records in Form view generally one record at a time. The last form in Form view is a blank record used for adding a new record. Note that forms may be extensively customized – the form illustrated in this section was created by Access using the Form Wizard.

Data entry using forms is the preferred way to populate a database. Forms have a rich set of controls which assist in data entry, data lookup, and data organization (such as tabs to cluster related information). Forms may also be customized to assist in data entry and to provide end users with detailed information and suggested corrective steps when a problem with data entry is encountered. Lastly, a form can contain one or more *subforms* which greatly assist in managing relational data (although one can also use **subdata sheets** in table datasheet view to achieve similar results). For example, a form with a single subform can be used to manage one-to-many data so you can view, edit, or enter data in both tables using a single data entry form. Creating such forms are discussed beginning on Page 114.

Points on Entering Data

- The data entered into each field must adhere to the declared data type and format of the field.
- Data entered into a primary key field must be unique. If the value matches that of an existing record Access will detect a record validation error. You will not be able to save the current record until the primary key violation is removed.

- Press **Tab** to advance to the next field and press *Shift + Tab* to return to the previous field.

- Records are automatically saved when you either move to another record or close the table. Although not required, you can manually save changes by selecting **Save** from the **Records** group of the **Home** ribbon.

- New records that are added to a table with a primary key field are automatically placed in sequence, based on the primary key field.

- For a table on the *one* side of a one-to-many join, you can open a *subdatasheet* to enter data in the related table. Subdatasheets behave exactly like standard tables. All the rules above apply to subdatasheets as well.

When viewing or editing records in either tables or forms, symbols in the following table will appear indicating the status of the record. For tables, these symbols appear in the **Record Status** column. For forms, the symbols will appear in the form's **Record Selector** bar.

Record Status Symbols

Symbol	Description
(color bar)	Indicates the current record. The record is being viewed and no editing is occurring.
✐	Indicates the record is being edited.
⊘	Indicates the record is locked. In a multi-user database, another individual is making changes to the record. Individuals who see the locked record indicator may not make edits to the record until the original editor has finished. When the record can be edited again, the Locked Record symbol is removed.
★	Indicates a new record. As soon as data entry begins in a new record this symbol changes to the record edit symbol.

In addition to the **Record Status** column, the **Record Navigator** also includes a control (far right in the following illustration) which will create a new record in either a table or form view.

Record: I◄ ◄ 1 of 1 ► ►I ►

How to Enter Data in the Datasheet View

An example of a table with a single record (and the insertion point in a new record) is illustrated below. The term *(New)* indicates that the field PID is associated with an autonumber. There is no need to enter data into that field as Access will automatically add the next number in sequence.

Step 1.   Open the table in **Datasheet** view.

Step 2.   Check to ensure that the insertion point is in the blank record, or click once on the blank record to place the insertion point.

Step 3.   Enter data into the first field.

Step 4.   Press *Tab* to move to the next field.

Step 5.   Enter data into the next field.

Step 6.   Repeat Steps 4 and 5 until all data has been entered.

 Pressing *Tab* in the last field in a record will move the insertion point to the first field of the next record and save the previous record. Press *Shift + Tab* to move to the previous field. Press *Ctrl + Enter* to insert a hard return in a memo field.

How to Enter Data in the Form View

An example of a form with a single record (and the insertion point in a new record) is illustrated below. The term *(New)* indicates that the field PID is associated with an autonumber. There is no need to enter data into that field as Access will automatically add the next number in sequence.

Step 1.   Open the form in **Form** view.

Step 2.   Use the **Record navigator** to create a new record, or from the **Records** group of the **Home** ribbon, select **New**.

Step 3.   Enter data into the first field.

Step 4.   Press *Tab* to move to the next field.

Step 5.   Enter data into the next field.

Step 6.   Repeat Steps 4 and 5 until all data has been entered.

 Press *Ctrl + Enter* to insert a hard return in a memo field.

Working with Subdatasheets

If a table has been joined to one or more tables using the **Relationship Window**, you can work with that table's related data using a *subdatasheet*. When the table from the *one* side of the join is open in **Datasheet** view, an **Expand Indicator** (+) will appear between the **Row Indicator** and the first column in the table. This control permits you to open the related table for the current record. You can add, edit, or delete data in the related table.

How to Open a Subdatasheet

The table from the *one* side of an established join must be open in **Datasheet** view. This procedure assumes that you have not established a subdatasheet.

Step 1.   Select any of the **Expand Indicators** (+) which appear to the left of the first
           field in the table. A dialog box similar to the following will appear.

Step 2.   Choose the desired table on the *many* side of the join (note that Access will list
           all available tables, not just those related to the current table).

Step 3.   Work with the data in the **subdatasheet** as you would any table in **Datasheet**
           view.

Step 4.   To close the **subdatasheet** select the **Collapse Indicator** (-) associated with
           the current record in the table on the *one* side of the join.

Step 5.   To open a **subdatasheet** for another record, select the **Expand Indicator** (+)
           for that row.

Deleting Data

You can delete data from fields or permanently delete records from a table or form. Once deleted,
a record cannot be retrieved. This is particularly significant when tables in the database are related
to one another. If deleting data from a table on the *one* side of a join and **cascade delete related
records** has been established, deleting a record will automatically cascade the delete to the related
table. Access will warn you before conducting this type of record deletion.

When creating a new record, either in a table or in a form, pressing *Esc*
once deletes the data in the current field. Pressing *Esc* a second time deletes
the entire record. When working with an existing record, pressing *Esc* once
deletes the most recent field data entry while pressing *Esc* twice has no
effect.

Unlike other members of the Microsoft Office suite, Access does not offer unlimited undo commands. If you delete a field the deletion can be undone if acted upon immediately. This is also true of a record that is not associated with other records via a cascade delete relationship. If you delete a record and close the table or form or move to another record there is no way to undo the original deletion.

How to Delete Data from a Field

Step 1.   Select the data.

Step 2.   Press the *Delete* key, or from the **Record** group of the **Home** ribbon, choose **Delete**.

How to Delete a Record from a Table

Step 1.   Select the record by choosing the **Record Selector** located at the far left of the record row (if using a form the record selector may be a vertical bar located on the form's left side).

Step 2.   Press the *Delete* key, or from the **Record** group of the **Home** ribbon, choose **Delete**.

If the record in the table is not related to records in other tables, the following dialog box will appear:

If the record in the table has related records in other tables and **cascade delete related records** has been set, the following dialog box will appear:

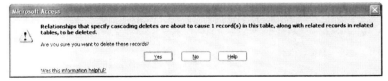

Step 3.   Select **Yes** to confirm that you want the record deleted, or select **No** to return to the table without deleting the record.

Importing Microsoft Excel Data into Access

It may not always be necessary to key data directly into a table. Access can import data from Excel, ODBC (open database connectivity) Databases, and files such as plain text, HTML, and XML. Data may be imported either into existing or new tables. Importing data directly into an Access table reduces data entry time and the possibility of data entry errors.

When Excel data are imported into Access – either into a new or an existing table – Access examines the first 8 rows of the Excel data in order to make decisions regarding data types. For example, if the first 15 rows in a column contain numeric data and the remaining rows in that column are formatted as dates, the date values will be converted into numbers when imported into Access.

 Importing data copies information from the source to the destination Access table. The original data are preserved.

Notes on Importing Data

Regardless of whether you are importing from a text file (which includes HTML and XML) or from an existing Excel workbook, there are a couple of considerations which must be addressed:

If importing into a new table

The data to be imported must be structured in a way that reflects the structure of a table. For plain text, HTML, and Excel worksheets this means that the data must exist in regular rows and columns. Particularly with Excel, there cannot be any subtotals or any formatting that breaks the regular, tabular structure. The imported data should not contain merged cells or any structure that violates the notion of a regular grid.

Access will attempt to apply the best data type to each column, depending upon the data. For example, if all data in a particular column look like dates, Access will create a Date/Time data type. However, if a single value in that column isn't a date, Access will default to a text data type.

If importing into an existing table

The structure of your imported data must match that of the table you are importing into. If you are importing from an existing Excel worksheet the column headings must exactly match the field names from the target table.

The data types of the Excel columns must match the data types of the columns in the Access table.

If any data in a column fails to meet the data type for the target column it will not be imported.

How to Import Excel Data into a New Access Table

Read the notes in the previous section before attempting to import data.

Step 1.   Begin the process by choosing **Excel** from the **Import & Link** group on the **External Data** ribbon.

Step 2.   In the **Get External Data – Excel Spreadsheet** dialog, select the file to import and keep the default setting **Import the source data into a new table in the current database.** Choose **OK.** The first dialog of the **Import Spreadsheet Wizard** will appear similar to the following:

Step 3.   If necessary, select the worksheet or named range to import, then choose **Next.**

Step 4.   In the second import wizard dialog box, indicate whether the first row in the worksheet contains field names. The third dialog box of the **Import Spreadsheet Wizard** will appear similar to the following:

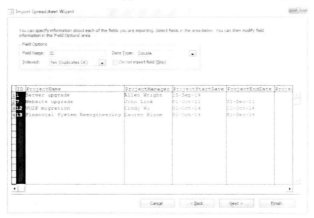

Step 5.   If your first row did not include field names, for each column you wish to import type a field name in the **Field Name** text box. Ensure that the datatype proposed fits the data and set an index (if desired). Note that you may also elect to not import any column. Select **Next** when ready.

Step 6.   In the next dialog box, choose a primary key (if desired). Use the following table as a guide to the options.

Primary Key Options

Option	Description
Let Access add primary key	Access will add an AutoNumber field to your table. Remember that such a primary key will not ensure non-duplicate data in the imported table.
Choose my own primary key	If the imported data has values that are unique (no duplicates) and serve to uniquely identify each row of data, then choose this option and use the drop-down list to identify the field.
No primary key	If the imported data lacks the conditions for a candidate primary key, or if you are unsure, choose this option. A primary key may be set later if required.

Step 7.   In the final dialog box name your imported table and choose **Finish**.

Step 8.   Optionally, you may choose to save the import procedure for quick reuse. Give the saved task a name and indicate whether you wish to also establish a task in

Microsoft Outlook (which can be set to alert you and/or become a recurring task).

 If you save the import procedure it will be listed in the **Saved Imports** folder, accessible from the **Import & Link** group on the **External Data** ribbon.

How to Import Excel Data into an Existing Access Table

If you import data into an existing Access table, that table must be closed before running this procedure. Read the notes in the previous section before attempting to import data. The order of columns, by data type, must exactly match between the Excel worksheet and the Access table. If the columns have column names (usually on Row 1) they must exactly match the field names in the Access table.

Step 1.   Begin the process by choosing **Excel** from the **Import & Link** group on the **External Data** ribbon.

Step 2.   In the **Get External Data – Excel Spreadsheet** dialog, select the file to import and choose **Append a copy of the record to the table.** From the drop down box select the target table, then choose **OK.** The first dialog of the **Import Spreadsheet Wizard** will appear similar to the following:

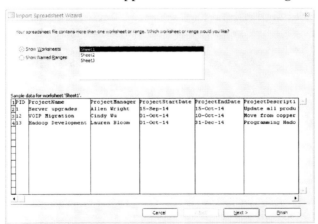

Step 3.   If necessary, select the worksheet or named range to import, then choose **Next**.

Step 4.   In the second import wizard dialog box, indicate whether the first row in the worksheet contains field names.

Step 5.   Select **Finish.**

Step 6.   Optionally, you may choose to save the import procedure for quick reuse. Give the saved task a name and indicate whether you wish to also establish a task in Microsoft Outlook (which can be set to alert you and/or become a recurring task).

Importing Text Data into Access

Many computer applications, including legacy databases, are capable of saving data in a plain text format. You can use such a text file to import the data into Access. This technique is useful when dealing with applications from different types of databases.

For the importation of text files to be successful, the text data must adhere to the following rules:

- Each field in the text file must be represented in some clear manner. There are two generally accepted protocols: *fixed width* (in which case each field occupies a set number of spaces) or *delimited* (in which case each field is separated from the next by some character, the most common being the tab character).

- Each record in the text file must also be represented in some clear manner. The standard is to separate each record by using a carriage return – line feed combination.

  The **Import Wizard** can generally determine the field and record separation protocols used, but you may need to consult with the administrator or owner of the original data if you encounter problems in importing the file.

How to Import Text Data into an Existing Access Table

Step 1.   Begin the process by choosing **Text** from the **Import & Link** group on the **External Data** ribbon.

Step 2.   From the **Get External Data – Text File** dialog box, select the file to import and choose whether to import to a new or an existing Access table. Choose **OK** when done. The second dialog box of the **Import Text Wizard** will appear similar to the following:

Step 3.   The wizard will attempt to determine how the fields in your data are identified (Delimited or Fixed). Ensure that the correct option has been selected, then choose **Next**.

If your data are delimited, a dialog box similar to the following will appear. You may need to adjust settings in order for the display to match your expectations of the structure of the columns.

If your data are in a fixed width format, a dialog box similar to the following will appear. You may need to adjust the point where each column (field) begins by adjusting arrows or creating or deleting arrows.

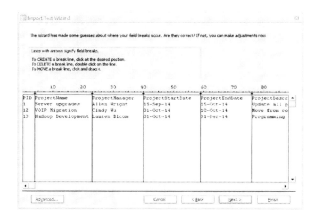

Step 4. In the next dialog box, adjust field name and data type and choose indexing properties (if desired). Optionally you can choose to omit any column from importation. Choose **Next** when done.

Step 5. Choose a primary key, if desired. Refer to the table on Page 87 for specifics. Choose **Next** when done.

Step 6. If importing into a new table, name the table and select **Finish**

Step 7. Optionally, you may choose to save the import procedure for quick reuse. Give the saved task a name and indicate whether you wish to also establish a task in Microsoft Outlook (which can be set to alert you and/or become a recurring task).

Warning: Importing text data into an existing table may generate import errors. If the text data violates validation rules or if the data types do not match correctly, some or all of the data will not be imported. In this case, Access will place the bad records in a table named **Import Errors**.

Troubleshooting Data Importing

There are some conditions that may create problems when you attempt to import data into Access. Under some circumstances, records that fail to be imported are documented in a table named **Import Errors**. This table will list the records that were not imported because of errors. The errors that can be documented are outlined in the following table.

Option	Description
Field Truncation	The **Field Size** property for the field is smaller than the imported data.
Type Conversion Error	The imported data is of the wrong data type for the field.
Key Violation	There is a duplicate in the table's primary key.
Validation Rule Failure	Imported data fails to pass a validation rule.
Null in Required Field	A field value is missing in a field with the **Required** property set to **True**.
Null Value in AutoNumber Field	The imported data contains a null in a field being mapped to an AutoNumber field in the database.
Unparsable Record	Imported data contains a series of nested double quotes. Access cannot determine the end of the field value (applies only to importation of text files).

 Warning: Violations involving input masks are not captured during the import process! If you receive errors in importing data and an **Import Errors** table is not generated, you may need to remove the destination table's input masks and then repeat the import process.

Strategies for Handling Import Errors

The following list serves as a general guide for handling import errors, which may assist in clearing up the most common import errors. However, it is not comprehensive, as many different types of errors may arise.

Imported Data Must Fit into a Regular Structure

- If importing worksheet data, the worksheet must consist of a regular array of rows and columns. Merged cells, header rows, and other formatting embellishments will cause errors.
- Text files must ultimately be structured so that every record in the text file has the same number of fields.

To fix this problem, perform the following:

- Carefully examine the structure of the worksheet you wish to import. Look for merged cells and heading or blank rows embedded in the array of data.
- When importing text files, you may need to consult the owner of the data to ensure that it is structured appropriately for import.

Imported Data must be of the Correct Data Type

- The incoming data must match the expected data type for every field in the table. For example, Access will not permit the importation of text data into a numeric or date/time field.

- When using an **Import Wizard** note that the wizard generally analyzes the first 8 rows of data and determines the data type.

To fix this problem, perform the following:

- Adjust cell format properties in Microsoft Excel to force columns of the worksheet to adopt the correct data type.

- Import the worksheet or text data into a new table and let Access determine and adjust the field data type. You can return to the table and adjust either the data and/or field data types and then **Paste Append** the data into the destination table.

Duplications or Null Values in a Primary Key Field are not Permitted

- Ensure that the incoming data does not contain duplicates, empty or null values in the field, or fields that will map to the destination table's primary key.

- Ensure that between the imported data and the existing data in the destination table there are no duplicated values in the field or fields that will map to the destination table's primary key.

- Use sorting tools in the application that contains the original data and manually scan the fields that will map to the destination table's primary key looking for either duplications or null values. Adjust field values as necessary.

- Import the data into a new table and when asked by the **Import Wizard** if you want to create or assign a primary key, indicate **No**. Refer to the procedures starting on page 53 for procedures to find null and duplicate field values.

 A best practice when importing data into an existing table is to first make a back up copy of the table. If the importation process yields unexpected or undesirable results you can restore the table to its original state by deleting the import table and restoring the backup copy table to its original name.

Chapter 6 | Queries

Formally, a query is a method for retrieving data from a database. The standard term for such a method is *Select Query*. Queries in Microsoft Access generally adhere to the *Structured Query Language* or *SQL*. Within the SQL specification (it is a standard language) falls a second class of queries known as *Action Queries*. So Access provides you with two broad categories of queryies: select queries ask specific questions of the data and action queries act on the data or the structure of the database. Both types of queries may involve multiple related tables. Select queries are the most common type of query as the general purpose of a database is to store useful information. Their usefulness is defined by the ability to ask questions and receive specific, factual answers. You'll see how to create select queries and to use *criteria expressions* to assist in formulating specific questions.

Action queries fall more into the category of utilities and are used to update or delete data within one or more tables, to append data into existing or new tables, or to create a table based in full or in part on an existing table.

In both cases, you'll use a graphical design tool to create queries, to add criteria expressions to narrow the results returned, and to modify the joins between tables to meet specific needs.

Select Queries

Select queries retrieve data from one or more tables, usually to satisfy a particular question (hence the generalized term *Query*). You can specify which fields the query will display and set criteria expressions (or search terms) for one or more fields. Criteria Expressions are discussed beginning on Page 101. If a select query is based on a single table, displays all of the table's fields, and has no criteria expressions, then it is analogous to viewing the table itself. Otherwise, the purpose of using a select query is to view a subset of the table's data.

Select queries always present their results in **Query Datasheet** view. All the sorting, filtering, and find operations available to tables and forms are also available to queries in **Query Datasheet** view.

Under some circumstances, the results of a select query are editable. This behavior is different from some other desktop database systems in which query results are statically displayed. If desired, you can specify that your select queries display static results as well, but note that the default behavior is to display the results dynamically.

The following points summarize select query features and usage:

- You can add *criteria expressions* to create highly selective queries that answer specific questions.

- Select queries may be based on one or more tables in the database. In a relational database, multi-table queries are one way to view related records across two or more tables.

- Select queries may be used to supply data to forms and reports, or to form controls such as combo or list boxes.

- Forms and reports that display data from two or more tables use queries to provide the data. This is true even for forms and reports created by wizards. Understanding queries means you can modify form and report designs more effectively.

 Select queries may summarize, total values, or apply arithmetic expressions. These features are beyond the scope of this book. Note that there is a separate book in this series titled Building Queries Using Microsoft Access which covers these topics in detail.

Action Queries

As their name suggests, action queries perform an operation on database tables. You can create a new table, or update, append, or delete data in existing tables. Action queries may run in one of two modes. The first permits you to view the data that will be acted upon if the query runs; the second actually runs the query. For example, if you intend to run a delete query to remove specific records from a table, you may first review the query results to see which records will be deleted, and then run the query.

The following points summarize action query features and usage:

- You can create a new table using a **Make Table** query.

- You can delete records in a table with a **Delete** query. You cannot delete the table itself with this query type, only the data the table contains.

- Existing records can be changed with an **Update** query.

- Records can be added to an existing table using an **Append** query.

- You can create, modify, or delete tables or issue commands to an OBDC (open database connectivity) database using **SQL-specific** queries. These are beyond the scope of this manual.

- Although there is no move query, you can pair an **Append** or **Make** Table and a **Delete** query to elicit the same effect.

- From the **Query Tools | Design** ribbon, the controls that elicit an action query are located in the **Results** group. The **View** button will show the records to be acted upon by the action query but will not run the query. The **run** button will run the query.

 Warning: The result of running an Action query cannot be undone. Under some conditions Access will let you view the data affected by an action query before it is run. See Page 100 for details.

Creating a New Query

Whether you intend to create a select or an action query, the starting point is the same.

How to Create a New Query

In this example we'll work with a query that is based on a single table. In a subsequent procedure we'll discuss working with related tables.

Step 1.   From the **Create** ribbon, in the **Queries** group, select **Query Design**.

Step 2.   From the **Show Tables** dialog box, add the table or tables you wish to include in the query, then choose **Close**. The **Query Design** area will appear similar to the following.

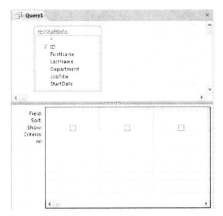

There are two working areas within the **Query Design** view. The upper area displays the one or more tables that the query will work on. The lower, **Criteria Grid** is where you add specific criteria in order to ask specific questions or in the case of action queries, to act upon specific data. This area also controls sort order and column visibility.

| Step 3. | Specify the type of query by choosing the appropriate option from the **Query Type** group on the **Query Tools | Design** ribbon. Use the following table as a guide. |

Type	Description
Select	Creates a query that asks a specific question of the data in one or more tables. This is the default new query type.
Make table	An action query that creates a new table based on an existing table.
Append	Adds data to an existing table (the source and target tables must have the same fields and data types). This is an action query.
Update	Changes data in an existing table. This is an action query.
Crosstab	A specialized query for creating summary views of data.
Delete	An action query that removes data from a table.
Union	Combine results from two or more select queries. This query type is not supported by Query Design view.
Pass-Through	Creates an SQL query that is submitted to an ODBC-compliant database for processing. Not supported by Query Design view.
Data Definition	Modify or create tables using SQL statements. Not supported by Query Design view.

How to Create a New Query Using a Wizard

Access provides several wizards to assist in the creation of a query. Of the available choices, the Simple Query Wizard is not much easier than following the previous procedure.

| Step 1. | From the **Create** ribbon, in the **Queries** group, select **Query Wizard**. |
| Step 2. | From the **New Query** dialog box, choose the type of Wizard using the following table as a guide. |

Option	Description
Simple Query Wizard	Starts a wizard that steps you through the process of creating a simple select query. You can create simple select queries or queries that summarize or total values, but you cannot create queries that use criteria expressions.
Crosstab Query Wizard	Summarizes (sums, counts, or averages) data in one field and groups the summaries by one set of data along the left and another set of data along the top. An example might be a summary of the count of all employees sent on each mission (left column), arranged by office (top row). It is a special case of the select query.
Find Duplicates Query Wizard	Finds duplicate values among fields. It is a useful option when attempting to find problematic primary keys in imported data, as you can quickly locate duplicates.
Find Unmatched Query Wizard	Automates the process of finding records among tables that violate referential integrity rules. It is a useful option when attempting to establish a relational join between tables of imported data.

Step 3.   Choose **OK**.

 If you select any of the query wizards, additional dialog boxes will appear and will step you through the process of creating your query. Once created, selecting **Design** view will open the **Query Design** view.

Query Design View

Query Design view is used to generate select and action queries from scratch or to work with queries created using a wizard. Working in this view you can add fields to the **Field Grid**, establish criteria expressions (discussed beginning on Page 101), and view query results. This view also provides the tools to change between query types. You can easily change from a select query to one of the action queries. Query Design view does not support union, pass-through, or data definition queries - for those queries you use SQL View instead.

When working with action queries, there is a difference between viewing the query results in **Datasheet** view and running the query. In the former case the query's specific action is not applied, but you can view the data that will be affected. In the latter case the action query is run.

The **Query Design** view is used to design the query. You add fields, set field properties, and enter criteria expressions in this view. The components of the **Criteria Grid** are explained in the following table.

Components of the Criteria Grid

Component	Description
Field	Lists a specific field name or the all fields indicator (*). The remaining components in this table will act on the field or fields named at the top of the column.
Table	Provides the name of the table containing the field. This is necessary for multiple table queries where there is a common field name between tables.
Sort	Sets sorting options: Ascending, Descending, or (not sorted).
Show	Controls whether the field appears in the result set.
Criteria	Specifies the one or more criteria expressions that may be used to filter the results. Criteria on the same row in different field columns are logically associated with the **AND** term.
Or:	As above, except when criteria are stacked vertically within the same field column the criteria are associated with the **OR** term
Total	Functions such as sum, average, max or min are available to summary queries (totals query only).
Append To:	Lists fields to append (append query only).
Update To	Lists fields to update (update query only).
Delete	Lists two SQL verbs: **Where** or **From**. The **Where** clause is used to add criteria to only delete specific records (delete query only).

How to Add Fields to Select Query

The procedure assumes you are in **Query Design** view.

Step 1.   In the **Table Area**, locate the table that contains the desired field and either double-click or drag the field to the next available field column in the **Criteria Grid**, or, in the field cell of the next available field column, choose the desired field from the drop down box. (Note for multiple table queries you may need to choose the table from the **Table** cell first.

When you drag a field you can place it between existing fields in the **Criteria Grid**. When you release the mouse button the dragged field will be inserted between the existing ones.

How to Remove Fields from a Query

This procedure assumes you are in **Query Design** view.

Step 1.   In the **Field Grid**, select the field to delete by positioning the cursor over the gray band immediately above the field name. When the mouse pointer becomes a downward pointing arrow, click once.

Step 2.   With the field column selected, press the *Delete* key.

How to Run a Query

As previously discussed, if you are working with any of the action queries, it is strongly advised that you run the query via the **View** button first. Once you're certain that the query is correct then all action queries must be initiated via the **Run** button to actually act on your data.

Step 1.   To view the results of a select or action query, select **View** from the **Query Tools** group of the **Query Tools | Design** ribbon, or, to run an action query, select **Run** from the **Query Design** toolbar.

 To return to the **Query Design** view, choose **View** from the **Home** ribbon.

 Warning: Selecting **Run** for an action query will cause the query to act upon the specified database objects. You cannot undo this action.

How to Save a Query

Step 1.   Select **Save** from the **Quick Access** toolbar.

Step 2.   In the **Save As** dialog box, type a new name. If desired, refer to Appendix A for suggested naming conventions.

Step 3.   Choose **OK**.

If you attempt to close an unsaved query, Access will prompt you to first save it.

Criteria Expressions

You can restrict the results of a select query, or limit the records affected by an action query, by creating criteria expressions. An expression is any combination of literal characters, operators, and/or functions that evaluate unambiguously to a true or false value. When you enter a criteria expression into the **Criteria** row of the **Field Grid**, Access will evaluate this expression for every record the query could potentially retrieve. Only records where the expression evaluates to **True** will be displayed.

Criteria expressions in Access are **case-insensitive**. In a criteria expression, the text *Smith*, *smith*, and *SmItH* will all resolve to the same results.

Using the Field Grid for Criteria Expressions

You will achieve different logical expressions depending on where you enter criteria expressions in the **Field Grid**. Use these rules when creating criteria expressions:

- Expressions entered in the **Criteria** or in the **or** row for any field column act only against the values in that field.

- Expressions entered in several fields, but all on the same **Criteria** or **Or** row, act together banded by the logical **AND** operator.

- Stacking expressions in the same field column, but in the **Criteria** and in the **Or** rows, relates the expressions together using the **OR** operator.

- Combining a mixture of expressions in various field columns and **Criteria** or **Or** rows creates more complex logical statements. The criteria in any given row are addressed as a logical unit and are evaluated first. Criteria between rows are connected using the **OR** operator and are evaluated after criteria in any given row are evaluated.

The following series of illustrations outline this behavior. For simplicity, only the effect for select queries will be discussed.

Placing a single expression in a single **Criteria** cell, as illustrated below, will return all records where the **State** value is equal to **DC**.

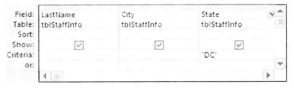

Placing expressions in *two* criteria cells *on the same row*, as illustrated in the next image, results in the display of all records where the **City** field is equal to **Bethesda** *AND* the **State** field is equal to **MD**.

As illustrated below, placing criteria in the same column but in the **Criteria** and the **Or** row results in a query that will return records where the **State** value is equal to **DC** *OR* the **State** value is equal to **VA**.

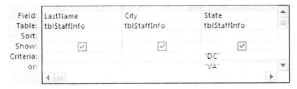

As shown below, placing two criteria in the same **Criteria** row but only one criteria in the **or** row results in an query that returns records where the **LastName** is equal to **King** *AND* the **State** is equal to **DC** *OR* all records where the **State** is equal to **VA**.

Lastly, creating a matrix where there are multiple criteria on both the **Criteria** row and the **or** row, as show in the following illustration, results in a query that returns records where the **LastName**

is equal to **King** AND the **State** is equal to **DC** *OR* the **LastName** is equal to **King** AND the **State** is equal to **VA**.

Literal Expressions

When you enter text, numeric, or date values into a **Criteria** cell, only records that exactly match your typed value will be displayed, or, if running an action query, will be acted upon.

Literal Expressions

Field Type	Comments
Text	Type the value as plain text. When you leave the criteria cell the value will automatically be enclosed in double quotes. If Access has trouble interpreting your text you may need to manually begin and end your text with double quotes. **Example:** "Peru"
Numeric	Enter the value as a regular number (omit currency symbols and thousands separators). **Example:** 74000 *or* 345.004
Date/Time	Enclose the date or time value in pound signs (#). Generally you can use any unambiguous date format. **Example:** #01/01/93# *or* #January, 01 1993#. Note that these two examples would retrieve the same records.

Operators and Wildcards

You can use operators or wildcards to provide a broader range of functionality to your criteria expressions. Operators are mainly mathematical symbols used for comparison and wildcards generally act as placeholders in your expressions.

Common Expression Operators

Operator	Name	Example
=	Equals operator	= "Pennsylvania"
<	Less than	< 500
<=	Less than or equals	<= 500
>	Greater than	>500
>=	Greater than or equals	>=500
<>	Not equal to	<> "Pennsylvania"
Null	Null (used for comparison)	<> Null (*reads "is not null"*)
Between	Between (for specifying date ranges)	Between #01/01/2010# AND #01/01/2013#

Common Expression Wildcards

Wildcard	Description	Examples
*	Matches any number of characters. May be placed at the beginning or the end of a text string.	wa* finds *Wabash, Washington.* *ton finds *Washington, Reston.*
?	Matches any single alphabetic character.	T?P finds *TAP, TIP,* and *TOP.*
[ ]	Matches any single character within the brackets.	T[AI]P finds *TAP* and *TIP* but not *TOP.*
!	Matches any single character *not* in the brackets.	T[!AI]P finds *TOP* but not *TAP* or *TIP.*
-	Matches any one of a range of characters. The range must be specified in ascending (A-Z) order.	T[I-Z]P finds *TIP* and *TOP.*
#	Matches any single numeric character. Only used in numeric fields.	5#5 finds *505, 515, 525,* etc.

 When you enter an expression containing a wildcard, the **Like** operator is automatically added to the beginning of your expression.

With the exception of the # symbol, wildcards are intended to be used in text fields only. If the international settings for the computer accept text in date values, you can use the * and ? wildcards when searching for month names.

 If you need to search for a character reserved as a wild card, enclose it in square brackets. **Example:** [?] will search for the question mark. To search for paired square brackets, enclose them in square brackets. **Example:** [[ ]] will search for empty square brackets.

Examples of Operator and Wildcard Expressions

Example	Description
>0 AND <=100	Finds values between 1 and 100, inclusive.
<=50 OR >=100	Finds values less than or equal to 50 *or* greater than or equal to 100.
>#01-Jan-2000#	Finds dates from January 02, 2000 and later.
Between #01/01/2011# AND #12/31/2013#	Finds dates that fall in the range between January 01, 2011 and December 31, 2013.
Like "Fin*"	Finds *Finance* and *Financial*.
Like "[a-d]*"	Finds values where the first character is either A, B, C, or D.

Query Join Types

When you work with two or more joined tables in a query, the type of join is indicated as a line that connects the table representations in the **Table Area** of the **Query Design** view. These join types may be modified and the modifications saved with the query.

Points on Query Join Types

- If you establish table relationship joins using the default *equi-join*, then all queries will also use the default join type. Joins are discussed starting on page 70.

- Modifying a join between tables in a query *does not* alter the join between tables as established in the **Relationships** window. For this reason it is preferred that joins are modified in queries.

- You may need to modify a one-to-many join in a query to ensure that all the records on the *one* side are displayed by the query, regardless of whether the *many* side has corresponding records. For example, producing a staff directory that also lists staff skills would require a query with a left join so all staff are listed, even those with no extra skills.

- Queries using either *left* or *right* joins are useful when troubleshooting errors in establishing referential integrity. This is discussed on page 74.

- When you modify a join in a query and then save the query, the modified join is also saved with the query.

How to Change a Query Join Type

When a query contains two or more tables and table joins have previously been established using the Relationships Window, the upper region of the query design area will display the joined tables in a manner similar to that when working with the Relationships Window.

Step 1.   In **Query Design** view locate the desired join and double-click. A dialog box similar to the following will appear:

Option	Description
Table Name	Changes the table that is on either the left or right side of the join. This option does not affect the join type and is not recommended.
Column Name	Changes the field in the left or right table that the join is based on. This is not a recommended option.
Join Option 1	Creates an *equi-join*, which is the default in most relational joins. Only matching records from both tables are displayed.
Join Option 2	Creates a *left join*. All records from the left table (the *one* side) and only those from the right table (the *many* side) that have matching records, are included.
Join Option 3	Creates a *right join*. All records from the right table (the *many* side) and only those records from the left table (the *one* side) that have matching records, are included.
New	Creates an entirely new join between any two tables or queries listed in the **Table Area**.

Step 2.   Adjust the join type as desired.

Step 3.   Choose **OK**.

 The type of join will be indicated graphically. An arrow-shaped join from one-to-many represents a left join, an arrow-shaped join from the many side to the one side represents a right join, and a join without arrows represents an equi-join.

Step 4.   Continue modifying the query design if desired and then run it to verify the results.

Step 5.   If desired, save the query. The modified join will be saved with the query design.

Modifying joins in queries is a better practice than modifying joins in the **Relationships** window. Query joins only affect the output of the query itself while joins modified in the **Relationships** window affect the entire database.

Working with Action Queries

Action queries are a special class of queries in that they perform specific actions that change the contents of a table, either by creating a new table, deleting records, appending data to a table, or updating data in a table. Once an action query has been run (as opposed to viewed) its action is irreversible. You may find it prudent to back up your database before running action queries.

Types of Action Queries

Name	Description
Make Table	Creates a new table. You must base the new table on one or more existing tables (or queries). Generally, the new table is also populated with data, depending on any criteria expressions present.
Append	Adds new records to an existing table. You can append fewer fields than the target table contains but all fields you append must match in both name and data type between the append query and the destination table.
Update	Changes the values in one or more fields of a table, depending on specific criteria expressions you create. A new row, **Update to**, appears in the **Field Grid**. Use this row to specify the new field values.
Delete	Deletes records from a table. Which records are deleted depends on any criteria expressions you create.

How to Create an Action Query

Step 1.   From the **Create** ribbon, in the **Queries** group, select **Query Design**.

Step 2.   From the **Show Tables** dialog box, add the table or tables you wish to include in the query, then choose **Close**.

Step 3   From the **Query** Type group, choose the desired action query.

Step 4.   For **Make Table** and **Append** queries, a dialog box will appear named after the action query you have selected. Choose an existing table in the current database (or for **Make Table** queries type the name of the new table), or, choose **Another database**, provide a file name, and then choose an existing table (or for **Make Table** queries, type the name of the new table).

Step 5.   Choose **OK**.

Step 6.   Modify the **Criteria Grid** if you wish to restrict the records which will be acted upon.

Step 7.   From the **View** group, select **View** to review the records the query will act on, or, select **Run** to run the action query.

Step 8.   If desired, save the query.

Chapter 7 | Forms

Forms make working with data in Access an easy task. Although you can use tables to enter or locate data, forms can be configured to focus on a single record at a time, thus permitting you to work with that data alone. Forms may also be used in conjunction with subforms so data from related tables may be displayed.

In this Chapter we'll briefly survey different types of forms and step through the procedure to quickly create a form based on a single table as well as on table data that models one-to-many and many-to-many joins.

Overview of Forms

Forms are used to display data from tables or queries. They can use sophisticated formatting and user interface controls and can display data in a variety of layouts. Forms are the preferred method of entering, editing, and viewing database data.

Features of forms include the following:

- Entering, editing, and saving data in forms involves procedures identical to that for tables.

- Sorting, finding, and filtering procedures are identical between forms and tables.

- Forms can display a single record, a few records, or like tables, many records at once.

- You can display data from related tables by adding *subforms* to a form. As you step through records on the form (displaying information from the *one* side of a relational join), the subform automatically updates to display the related records (from the *many* side of the join). You can edit the data in either the form or the subform. Forms can contain several subforms.

- Forms are most easily created using the **Form Wizard**. The design of any form may be modified using Form Design view.

- *Controls* can be added to forms, or existing controls changed to other useful types. Controls can simplify the display and editing of data, or they can provide added functionality to the form.

 Forms are complex objects. Their manual creation and modification will not be considered in this book. Note, however, that there is a separate book in this series titled Building Forms and Reports Using Microsoft Access.

Types of Forms

Not all forms are necessarily used to display data. A form that displays data from a table or query is said to be *bound* to a *data source*. Forms may be *unbound* as well. In the latter case they are typically used for general and administrative purposes such as menus, log-on dialog boxes, etc.

The various wizards and predefined forms in Access are all *bound* forms. To create an unbound form you'll need to work directly in **Form Design** view. The following table outlines each of the options available from the **Forms** group on the **Create** ribbon.

Form Options

Option	Description
Form	Creates a quick form based on the currently selected table or query.
Form Design	Opens a blank form in the form design view.
Blank Form	Opens a blank form in form view.
Form Wizard	Creates one or more forms based on the table or related tables you select. This is a very useful way to quickly create a working form, especially for one-to-many relationships.
Navigation	Creates a tabbed area that serves as a container for other forms you've created. There are options for placement of tabs and the form area.
More forms – Multiple Items	Creates a form that displays multiple records, but unlike the datasheet form, may also contain form controls within the data display area.
More forms – datasheet	Creates a form that displays data in datasheet view. The form header and footer area may contain form controls.
More forms – split form	A form that contains an area that displays a single record as well as an area that displays a datasheet view of the underlying table.
More forms – modal dialog	Creates a form with some preset properties to make a modal dialog box. Modal boxes demand your attention. No other Access object may be manipulated until a modal dialog box is closed.
More forms – PivotChart	Creates a form that displays a PivotChart.
More forms – PivotTable	Creates a form that displays a PivotTable.

Form Views

Access differentiates between three separate views when working with forms: Form View, Layout View, and Design View. When working with a form, these views are available from the **Views** group, located on either the **Home** or the **Form Layout Tools | Design** ribbons. Their features are described below.

Form Views

Type	Description
Form	This is the working version of the form. If the form is *bound* the underlying data are displayed.
Layout	An intermediate step between form and form design views, Layout lets you make some design changes while still viewing data. In layout view you can see how your data will appear as you make design changes.
Form Design	This view is for making all detailed design changes to a form. The form is "disconnected" from the data in that you cannot view data, only the controls, form sections, and their properties.

Overview of Form Creation

Of all the ways to create a new form in Access, the **Form Wizard** is the most useful. The Form Wizard gives you control over which fields are used to display as well as the general layout of the fields on the form. Importantly, the wizard can create forms based on both one-to-many and many-to-many relationships, provided you defined these relationships using the **Relationships window**. Frequently, developers first create a form using the **Form Wizard** and then modify the form design manually to add additional functionality.

Forms that are bound to a single table represent the simplest type of data entry forms. When a form is bound to two or more tables, or to a query that itself displays data from several tables, another layer of complexity is added because the form will typically contain one or more subforms. A subform is necessary in order to show the zero to many records from the related table. This topic will be addressed later in this chapter.

How to Create a Simple Form

We will use the **Form Wizard** to create a simple form, although you can quickly create such a form by selecting a table and choosing **Form** from the **Form** group of the **Create** ribbon. One problem with this approach is that any Autonumber primary key fields will be displayed on your form. This may confuse people who conduct data entry as the field will be editable when it really shouldn't be. Using the Wizard gives you greater control over your form design.

Step 1.   From the **Create** ribbon, in the **Forms** group, choose **Form Wizard.** A dialog box similar to the following will appear.

Step 2.   Choose a table or query (based on a single table) from the **Tables/Queries** drop-down list.

Step 3.   The **Available Fields** area will list the fields from the selected table or query. Use the **>** button to move individual fields to the **Selected Fields** area (the **>>** button will move all fields). In this example, we'll move all but the **ID** field. It's presence isn't necessary for a data entry form as it is associated with an autonumber field.

    The **Remove** button (**<**) and the **Remove all** button (**<<**) are used to remove a selected field or all fields, respectively, from the list of selected fields.

Step 4.   Choose **Next**. A dialog box similar to the following will appear:

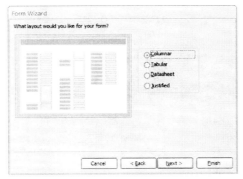

Step 5.   Choose a layout option. The following table outlines the choices.

Option	Description
Columnar	The form displays one record at a time with fields arranged in columns. Data labels are to the left of their accompanying text box.
Tabular	The form displays many records at a time. A header area contains the field labels and under each label a column of fields associated with several records is shown. Each row of data corresponds to one record.
Datasheet	The records are displayed in a form exactly as they would be in datasheet view of a table. This type of form is generally used when you intend to embed the datasheet form in another form.
Justified	A variation of the columnar option. Labels are placed above their corresponding text areas and fields are arranged across the form such that one or more rows of fields occupy the full width of the form yet only display data for one record at a time.

Step 6.   Choose **Next** when done. The final dialog box for the **Form Wizard** will appear similar to the following:

Step 7.   Provide a name for your new form. Good naming conventions for objects such as forms are discussed in Appendix A.

Step 8.   Select whether to open your form for data entry or open it in design view for further design.

Step 9.   Choose **Finish**.

Forms and One-to-Many Joins

The **Form Wizard** makes creating forms that display data from related tables relatively easy. You have a choice between viewing data from the *many* side of a join in a subform or on a linked (pop-up) form.

Points on Creating a Form to Display One-to-Many Related Data

- Before using the **Form Wizard**, it is important that the required relational joins have already been established in the **Relationships Window**.

- Although the form can be bound to a query that supplies data from two related tables, this is not necessary. You can select fields from two related tables using the wizard.

- The form can display the data from the *many* side of the join either as a subform or as a linked form (which act as pop-up forms). The general design rule is to use a subform if space on the main form permits and if there is an immediate need to view the related records. Use a linked form if space is at a premium or if there is only occasional need to view the related records.

- When using a form that contains a subform, there will be two sets of **Record Navigator** controls. The outermost set controls movement of the records on the main form (the *one* side of the join) while the inner set controls movement through the subform records (the *many* side of the join).

- When using a form that calls a linked form to display the related records, the linked form maintains synchronization with the main form. As you move between records on the main form (the *one* side of the join), the records in the linked form will update to display the related records (the *many* side of the join).

How to Create a Form to Display One-to-Many Related Data

Step 1.   From the **Create** ribbon, in the **Forms** group, choose **Form Wizard.** A dialog box similar to the following will appear.

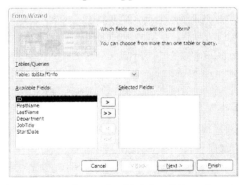

Step 2.   Choose a table or query from the **Tables/Queries** drop-down list. If working with tables, select the table from the *one* side of the *one-to-many* relation join first.

Step 3.   The **Available Fields** area will list the fields from the selected table or query. Use the **>** button to move individual fields to the **Selected Fields** area (the **>>** button will move all fields).

Step 4.   Return to the Tables/Queries control and select the table from the many side of the join. Repeat Step 3 to choose the desired fields from the second table. (If you are working with a query based on the two tables, ignore this step and simply add the desired fields while in Step 3).

 Unless you have a specific need to include the primary and foreign key fields know that their presence isn't necessary for the **Form Wizard** to create the proper form/subform arrangement. The wizard uses information about the relation join from the **Relationships Window**.

Step 5.   Choose **Next**. The second dialog box of the **Form Wizard** will appear similar to the following:

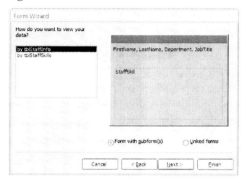

Step 6.   Select the format for the presentation of the related data by selecting either **Form with subform(s)** or **Linked forms**. Choose **Next**.

 The preview area should graphically acknowledge your intent by illustrating fields from the *one* side on the image of the main form and fields from the *many* side of the join on the subform or linked form. If the preview is incorrect, select another table in the **How do you want to view your data?** list box.

 If by choosing each of the listed tables the wizard fails to show the appropriate display of one-to-many records you may have either (1) selected an inappropriate table in Steps 2-4 or (2) the relationship between the tables may not be established correctly. In this case, refer to Chapter 4.

If you choose **Form with subform(s)** in the previous step, a dialog box similar to the following will appear:

Step 7.   Select **Tabular** to view columns of fields or **Datasheet** to view the subform data in a datasheet. Choose **Next** when done. The final dialog box of the **Form Wizard** will appear similar to the following.

Step 8.   Type a name for the form and subform. If desired, refer to Appendix A for suggested naming conventions. Choose **Finish.**

You do not need to include the primary or foreign key fields when designing forms in order for the related records to be synchronized. If the forms will be used to enter new records, however, the primary key must be present (unless it is an AutoNumber field) so its value can be entered. The foreign key in the subform or linked form will automatically be updated, regardless of whether it is present on the form.

A completed form would appear similar to the following:

Note the presence of two **Record Navigator** controls. The outer (lower-most) control steps through the main form (the *one* side of the join, in this case Staff) while the inner **Control** steps through any related records on the subform (representing the *many* side of the join, in this case, Staff Skills).

Forms and Many-to-Many Joins

The **Form Wizard** can create a form that displays data from tables joined in a many-to-many relationship. An issue, however, is whether to include fields from the *bridge table*.

Points on Creating a Form to Display Many-to-Many Related Data

- It is not necessary to include the primary and/or foreign key fields from any of the tables provided that the intended use of the form is for viewing or editing existing data. In this configuration, however, you cannot add new records.

- If you do not include foreign key fields from the bridge table, you can edit existing records on either side of the join but you cannot enter new records on either side of the join.

- Including the foreign key fields (which match the primary key fields from *both* tables) permits you to enter new records from either side of the join. However, you will need to manually enter the appropriate primary and foreign key values in the appropriate fields. Creating a new record in any table will still be contingent on the presence of validation rules, required fields, etc.

 There are advanced solutions to the problem of creating a many to many form that permits full and easy data entry, but it is beyond the scope of this book. This topic is discussed in the Building Forms and Reports using Microsoft Access book.

How to Create a Form to Display Many-to-Many Related Data

This procedure is fundamentally similar to that for creating a form to display one-to-many related data.

Step 1.   Follow the general procedure for creating a form to display one-to-many related data on page 114.

Step 2.   From the **New Form** dialog box, choose the table that represents one of the tables on the *many* side of the join.

Step 3.   Start the **New Form** wizard.

Step 4.   Add the desired fields from the table selected in Step 2.

Step 5.   While still viewing the first dialog box of the **Form Wizard**, select the other table from the *many* side of the join and add the appropriate fields.

Step 6.   If desired, select the bridge table and add the foreign key fields. Review the issues outlined on the previous page if necessary.

Step 7.   Proceed with the remaining dialog boxes of the **Form Wizard** as usual.

Chapter 8 | Reports

Like forms, reports are essential to making data in a database accessible. Reports organize database data for printing and in Access can be configured to also group data from one or more tables. Unlike forms, reports can be configured to summarize numeric or currency data as well, providing you with sub and grand totals based on any grouping levels you choose.

In this Chapter we'll review the basic types of reports available in Microsoft Access. We'll also step through the procedures to create simple reports, mailing labels, and reports that group and summarize data across several tables.

Overview of Reports

Reports are used to print data contained in the database. A report may simply yield a hard copy of a table's contents, may be specialized for tasks such as creation of mailing labels, or may represent a sophisticated summary of related records.

Features of reports include the following:

- Simple reports, based on a single table, can easily be created. Simple reports may use *grouping* to band similar records together. For example, to group staff by department. Grouping may be based on a field or fields within a single table or may represent fields across multiple tables.

- Mailing label reports are customized to print on a wide variety of label and paper types.

- Reports may be based on two or more related tables. A **Report Wizard** can quickly create *banded* reports that will print all of the related records (from the *many* side of the join) for each single record from the *one* side of the join. This feature also works for tables related in a many-to-many join.

- A subset of the *banded* report is the *groups/totals* reports. These not only band or group related data but can also summarize or total numeric values within groups and across the entire report.

 Reports are complex objects. Their manual creation and modification will not be considered in this book. Note, however, that there is a book in this series titled Building Forms and Reports Using Microsoft Access.

Types of Reports

The various types of reports you can create are summarized in the following table.

Type	Description
Simple	A report that is *bound* to the contents of a single table. If numeric data is present you can add a summary section to total the values.
Group/Total	A report generally *bound* to one or more related tables. For any given record from the *one* side of a join, the report will group or band the related records from the *many* side (this holds true also for many-to-many related tables). Within each group or band, if numeric data is present, you can add a summary section to total values. A summary section may also be added at the end of the report to create a grand total or grand summary.
Mailing Label	A specialized form of the simple report that is *bound* generally to a single table and is formatted to print in multiple columns to match popular mailing label formats.
Chart	Places an embedded chart object on a report. The chart uses data from the database as its source, but cannot produce multi-page reports that group charts.
Unbound	Reports in this group are not connected to a table or query. They may contain *subreports*, which are used to print groups of unrelated data, or they may simply be used to print generalized items such as coversheets, instructions, etc.

Overview of Report Creation

As with form creation, the easiest way to create a report is to use the **Report Wizard**. There are two report wizard types in Access:

- **Report Wizard** creates reports based on single or multiple, related tables. If the wizard senses that tables are related, it will suggest a grouped report format. If numeric data is present, you can elect to include summary information too.

- **Label Wizard** is used to step through the process of creating mailing labels.

There is also a AutoReport available in Access. It quickly creates a report based on a single table or query.

Grouped Reports

You can create reports that band or group records that share a common value in a selected field. Grouped reports can be created from single tables or from multiple, related tables. In the latter case, the grouping is typically arranged around the one-to-many or many-to-many relationship. In a single table, for example, one that stores employee information, you may choose to group on the **Department** field. This would produce a report that looks like a departmental directory, arranging employees in departmental groups.

Summary Reports

If numeric, currency, or yes/no fields are present in a report, the **Report Wizard** can create summary or totals fields. For simple reports, these fields will represent grand totals or summaries and will be placed at the end of the report. For grouped reports, the wizard can also include grouped totals or summaries as well.

Creating a Simple Report

Reports that are bound to a single table represent the simplest type of report. When a report is bound to two or more tables, or to a query that displays data from several tables, another layer of complexity is added since the **Report Wizard** will suggest grouping levels to display related records. Note that simple reports based on single tables may also use grouping.

How to Create a Simple Report using the Report Button

This method quickly creates a basic report. Any report can be further modified, although working in report design view is beyond the scope of this book.

Step 1.   Select the table you wish to base the report on.

Step 2.   From the **Create** ribbon, select **Report** in the **Reports** group. A quick report will be created and will appear in **Layout View**.

Step 3.   If desired, adjust column widths and/or make design changes to the report.

Step 4.   To print the report, from the **File** ribbon choose **Print**.

Step 5.   To save the report, choose **Save** from the **Quick Access** toolbar.

How to Create a Simple Report using the Report Wizard

The Report Wizard makes it easy to create simple reports that include grouping or order information based on one or more fields. In this example, we'll create a simple report from a staff table and group individuals by department.

Step 1. From the **Create** ribbon, select **Report Wizard** from the **Reports** group. A dialog box similar to the following will appear:

Step 2. If the desired table or query isn't selected, choose it from the **Tables/Queries** drop down box.

Step 3. To include fields on the report, move them from the **Available Fields** area to the **Selected Fields** area. Choose **Next** when done. The second dialog box of the Report Wizard will appear similar to the following:

Step 4. If grouping is desired, select the field or fields you wish to group. In the illustration above, *Department* has been selected as a group. The report will list each department and group employees associated with each department. Choose **Next** when ready.

 The **Grouping Options** button gives you more control over how groups are arranged. For example, if you group by a date/time field use **Grouping Options** to choose whether you group by absolute date, month, quarter, year, etc.

The third dialog box of the Report Wizard will appear similar to the following:

Step 5.   If you wish to order detail records (in this example, the detail records are grouped by department), select up to 4 fields. The **Ascending** button is a toggle. Choosing it will alternative between **Ascending** and **Descending** order. Select **Next** when ready. The forth dialog box of the Report Wizard will appear similar to the following.

Step 6.   Choose the layout and page orientation for your report. Use the following table as a guide to the three layout options. Select **Next** once your layout has been selected.

Option	Description
Stepped	Column headings appear at the top of a group, and any group headings appear on a line separate from any detail records.
Block	Like the stepped layout except each group heading appears in line with the detail records. This report is more compact and may require less paper to print.
Outline	Like the stepped layout except for detail records the column headings appear on a line below a group label and above any detail records. This report type may be easier to read but may also require more paper to print.

For reports that include many columns it may be advised to change the paper orientation to Landscape. Generally it is always a good idea to keep the **Adjust the field width so all fields fit on a page** option selected.

Step 7.   In the final Report Wizard dialog box provide a name for your report. (If desired, refer to Appendix A for suggested naming conventions.) The radio buttons let you choose whether to preview the report or open it in design view. Select **Finish** when you are done.

Reports and Related Tables

If you use the **Report Wizard** to create reports bound to two or more related tables (or which use a query that pulls data from two or more related tables), the wizard will create a *grouped* report.

A grouped report will group related records into as many as four levels. Records that share common values in the grouped field will be grouped together on the report.

Constructing reports that display information from tables involved in many-to-many joins is simpler than when constructing similar forms. Frequently, it is not necessary to include any fields from the bridge table unless specifically needed.

How to Create a Report from Related Tables

This process is similar to using the Report Wizard for single tables. When you add two or more tables the Report Wizard includes an additional dialog box. In this example we'll create a report that lists staff assigned to specific projects. The relationship between the various tables is illustrated below. Note that this is a *many-to-many* join. We'll include the field *budget* from the bridge table (it assigns a specific amount each staff is authorized to spend on a given project assignment). We'll use this information to tally the total budgeted amount for each project and for all projects across the enterprise.

Step 1. From the **Create** ribbon, select **Report Wizard** from the **Reports** group. A dialog box similar to the following will appear:

Step 2. Begin by working with the table on the *one* side of a *one-to-many* join, or if working with a *many-to-many* relationship, start with the table of greatest interest. If the desired table or query isn't selected, choose it from the **Tables/Queries** drop down box.

Step 3. Include fields from the primary table on the report, move them from the **Available Fields** area to the **Selected Fields** area.

Step 4. Return to the **Tables/**Queries drop down box and select the next table or query (generally a table on the *many* side of the join).

Step 5. Repeat Step 3 by adding the desired fields to the report. Choose **Next** when done.

 In this example, we're including ProjectName, ProjectManager, Start and End dates from the projects table, budget from the ProjectStaffing (Bridge) table, and Staff First and Last name, Department, and Job Title from the staff table.

The second dialog box of the Report Wizard will appear similar to the following:

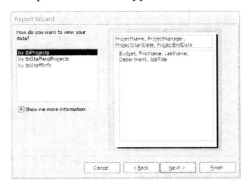

Step 6.   If the desired *one-to-many* or *many-to-many* relationship isn't displayed, select the alternative view using the **How do you want to view your data?** area. Choose **Next** when ready.

Step 7.   If grouping is desired, select the field or fields you wish to group. In this example, *Department* has been selected as a group. Under each project, the report will list each department and group employees associated with each department. For each employee the report will then list any associated skills. Choose **Next** when ready.

The *Detail* section of a report represents the lowest level of grouping. In the report being defined here, the grouping is first by Project, then by Department. Within each Department listing are the report details – here being staff. In the example, we've chosen to arrange the detail records alphabetically by staff last name.

Step 8.   If the wizard senses that any of the fields are numeric (including currency), or Yes/No data types, the **Summary Options** button will appear. In this example, select **Summary Options** to set how to summarize the budget field information. The Summary Options dialog box will appear similar to the following:

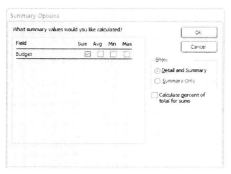

Step 9.   To include budget totals for each Project and for all projects, check the **Sum** checkbox and accept the default setting in the **Show** area. Choose **OK** when done. When you're returned to the Report Wizard, choose **Next** to continue.

Step 10.   Choose the layout and page orientation for your report. Select **Next** once your layout has been selected.

 For reports that include many columns it may be advised to change the paper orientation to Landscape. Generally it is always a good idea to keep the **Adjust the field width so all fields fit on a page** option selected.

Step 11.   In the final Report Wizard dialog box provide a name for your report. (If desired, refer to Appendix A for suggested naming conventions.) The radio buttons let you choose whether to preview the report or open it in design view. Select **Finish** when you are done.

In the example we've worked through, a portion of the report would appear similar to that illustrated below:

Project Name	Website upgrade			
Project Manager	John Link			
Start Date	·	01-Oct-11		
End Date		31-Dec-11		
Department	Finance			
LastName		FirstName	JobTitle	Budget
Smith		Amanda	Director	$1,500.00
Summary for 'Department' = Finance (1 detail record)				
Sum				$1,500.00
Department	IT			
LastName		FirstName	JobTitle	Budget
Jones		Jennifer	Support Tech	$1,500.00
Kidwell		Michael	Director	$1,500.00
Summary for 'Department' = IT (2 detail records)				
Sum				$3,000.00
Summary for 'ID' = 7 (3 detail records)				
Sum				$4,500.00

Note that for the Website Upgrade project, two departments – Finance and IT are involved. Finance has a single assigned staff (Amanda Smith) and she has been given a budget of $1,500 for the project. Thus the total department budget for this project is also $1,500.

The IT department has two staff assigned to this project, and each has been given a budget of $1,500. The total IT department budget for this project is $3,000 and the total project budget (located at the bottom of the illustration) comes to $4,500.

Mailing Label Reports

Another useful wizard is the **Label Wizard.** You can create mailing labels formatted for a wide variety of mailing label types, or create custom mailing label reports.

How to Create a Mailing Label Report

Step 1.   From the **Create** ribbon, in the **Reports** group, select **Labels**. The first dialog box of the **Label Wizard** will appear similar to the following:

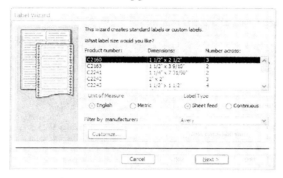

Step 2.   Choose a commercially available label from the **Filter by manufacturer** drop-down list, or, choose **Customize** to define a custom label size.

 Creating custom labels is a powerful feature but requires detailed knowledge of print layout. Whenever possible it is highly recommended that you use a commercially-available label.

Step 3.   From the **Which label size would you like?** area select the desired label. Choose **Next** when done. Note that the remainder of this procedure assumes that you are working with commercially available mailing labels. The second dialog box of the **Label Wizard** will appear similar to the following:

Step 4.   Select the desired properties to adjust the text appearance. Choose **Next** when done. The third dialog box of the **Label Wizard** will appear similar to the following:

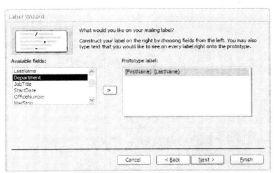

Step 5.   Use the **Available fields** area to select and move fields over to the **Prototype label** area. Note that you will need to manually enter spaces (such as between a first and last name field). Also you will need to manually enter a new line by pressing *Enter* when needed. The diagram of the label area roughly approximates the label and font sizes you selected in the previous steps. When your label prototype has been completed, select **Next** to continue.

Step 6.   Use the next dialog box to enter one or more fields you'll use to sort your labels. For example, if creating a bulk mailing for delivery in the United States, you'll want to sort by zip code. Choose **Next** when ready.

Step 7.   Lastly, name your label report and choose whether to view the label report in print preview or report design view. Choose **Finish** to complete the process.

Appendix A | Managing Database Objects

Your database is a complex object. Employing a good naming convention early on will make any future modifications to your design easier. This appendix touches on naming conventions as well as general maintenance tasks associated with an Access database.

Naming Conventions

Naming a database object is an important task. Frequently databases survive longer than anticipated. By employing a good naming convention, your objects "self-declare" what their purpose is. This makes future development or maintenance of the database an easier task.

Points on Naming Database Objects

- Although you can include blank spaces in an object name, some database systems that may interact with your Microsoft Access database objects may not be able to process object names containing spaces. If you anticipate that your database will interact with other database systems, or may be migrated to another database environment, you may want to keep blank spaces out of object names.

- Many developers use a system of a three-letter prefix to indicate the type of object. Refer to the following table for suggested object prefixes.

- Objects may be renamed in your database, but doing so, when other objects such as queries, forms, and reports refer to the renamed object, (such as a table), may cause problems. It is generally good practice to carefully name objects when they are created and stick to the name.

Object	Prefix	Examples
Table		
Standard	tbl	tblEmployees
Lookup	tblkup	tblkupStatePostalCodes
Query		
Append	qryapp	qryappAddNewEmployees
Crosstab	qryxtb	qryxtbLanguagesbyDepartment
Delete	qrydel	qrydelDeleteCompletedProjects
Select	qry	qryMissionStaffing
Summary	qrysum	qrysumCountofStaffbyDepartment
Make Table	qrymktbl	qrymktblCreateBackupEmployeeTable
Update	qryupd	qryupdUpdateFiscalYear
Form		
Lookup	frmlkup	frmlkupLookupDepartments
Standard	frm	frmMainMenu
Subform	sbfrm	sbfrmStaffLanguages
Report		
Standard	rpt	rptMissionStaffing
Subreport	sbrpt	sbrptStaffEducationalRecords
Macro	mcr	mcrImportExcelCountryData
Module	bas	basGeneralProcedures

 There are other naming conventions available. What is more important than your choice of a naming convention is the consistency with which you name your database objects.

General Maintenance Tasks

In Access, you can rename, copy, or delete any database object. You can also import database objects from one database into another.

When you rename a database object, Access by default is configured to cascade the new object name throughout the database using a feature called **Name AutoCorrect**. This is important if the renamed object, for example a table, is referenced by queries, forms, and reports. Without this feature enabled, the queries, forms, and reports based on a renamed table will be unable to work as expected because they are bound to the old table name.

Name AutoCorrect also works for fields within a table. Changes are automatically cascaded to any query, form or report that references the field. Note however that **Name AutoCorrect** does not cascade changes to macros or to VBA code, thus depending upon the complexity of your database it may be advised to limit name changes to the very early stages of database design.

How to Enable Name AutoCorrect

Name AutoCorrect is enabled by default for databases created in Access 2002 and later. For databases created in earlier versions and converted, you should follow this procedure to turn **Name AutoCorrect** on.

Step 1.   Select the **File** ribbon, then choose **Options.**

Step 2.   Select **Current Database**.

Step 3.   Move to the **Name AutoCorrect Options** area and check **Track name AutoCorrect info.**

Step 4.   Choose **OK**.

 If you also check **Log name AutoCorrect changes**, Access will create a table named **AutoCorrect Log** that will document name changes. This may be a useful tool if several people are developing the same database project. This feature does consume resources so ensure that it is turned off prior to your database entering full use.

 Warning: **Name AutoCorrect** will fix name changes to tables and their fields, queries, forms and their controls, and reports and their controls. It will not fix references in SQL statements. This is significant because forms or reports created using a wizard may use SQL statements as the data source. In this situation, the changed object name will not be fixed and those forms and reports will fail to work correctly.

 The best work practice is to think carefully about database object names and refrain from renaming objects once you have started the process of building your database.

How to Rename a Database Object

Step 1.   Select the object to rename from the **Shutter bar** area.

Step 2.   Right-click on the object and choose **Rename** from the shortcut menu.

Step 3.   Type a new object name, then press *Enter*.

How to Copy a Database Object

Step 1.   Select the object to copy from the **Shutter bar** area.

Step 2.   Right-click on the object and choose **Copy** from the shortcut menu.

Step 3.   Click once in the **Shutter bar** area (not on an existing object).

Step 4.   Right-click and choose **Paste** from the shortcut menu.

Step 5.   If you are copying any database object other than a table, type the name of the copy in the **Paste As** box and choose **OK**. This completes this procedure.

Step 6.   If you are copying a table object, the following dialog box will appear:

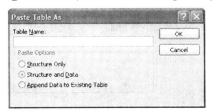

Paste Table Options

Option	Description
Structure Only	Copies the table structure only. The pasted copy will not contain any records.
Structure and Data	Makes a complete copy of the table, including any records contained in the original.
Append Data to Existing Table	Appends the data from the copied table to a table specified in the **Table Name** text box.

Step 7.   Choose a **Paste Option** and type a name for either the new table object or, in the case of appending data to an existing table, type the name of the existing table.

Step 8.   Choose **OK**.

If you create a copy of a table that maintains joins to other tables, only the table and/or its data are copied. The copy of the original table will not inherit any join specifications.

How to Delete a Database Object

Step 1.   Select the object from the **Shutter bar** area.

Step 2.   Right-click on the object and choose **Delete** from the shortcut menu.

 Warning: You cannot undo the deletion of any database object.

Points on Deleting Joined Tables

Access will not permit you to delete any table that is joined to another table without first removing the relationship join. Attempting to delete such a table will result in a message box similar to the following:

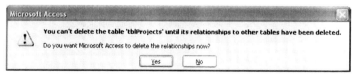

Choosing **Yes** will remove the relationship and delete the table. Choosing **No** will abandon the table deletion.

Deleting a table joined to other tables with referential integrity enforced (cascade deletions) **does not** delete the records from the related tables. Referential integrity is enforced only when records, either individually or in groups, are deleted. Deleting a table is considered an action apart from the process of maintaining referential integrity.

How to Import Database Objects

Any database object can be copied from one database into another. When importing tables it is important to note that the default is to also import table relationships. You can choose to omit importing relationships as an option.

Step 1.   Open the database intended to receive the imported database objects, or, create a new blank database.

Step 2.   From the **External Data** ribbon, choose **Access** from the **Import & Link** area.

Step 3.   In the **Get External Data** dialog box, navigate as necessary to locate the database containing the desired objects.

Step 4.   Choose either the **Import Tables..** or **Link to the data source...**option. Importing will bring a copy of the object(s) into your database. Linking creates a reference to the object(s) but does not import them. Select **OK** when done.

If importing objects the import Objects dialog box will appear similar to the following:

Step 5.   Select the desired objects to import, then choose **OK.** This completes the import procedure. The imported objects will appear in the appropriate object list in your current database. The remaining part of this discussion focuses on linking objects.

If Linking Objects the **Link Tables** dialog box will appear similar to the following:

Step 6.   Select the table or tables to link, then choose **Ok**.

 If you import objects that have the same name as existing objects in the current database, the imported objects will have a sequential number added to their names (for example, tblEmployees1). You should rename such objects to make their purpose more clear.

 A linked table will appear in the **Shutter bar** with a small link arrow next to the table icon. You cannot enter design view on a linked table. To modify the table design you must open the table in its source database.

Documenting Database Objects

Documentation of the objects in a database is an important task. It provides an outline of the structure of the database, which is extremely useful when future modifications of the design are required.

There are three complementary approaches to documenting your database:

- Name all database objects in a consistent and meaningful manner. Employ prefixes to identify the type of database object and then provide a name that declares the purpose or function of the object. At the table level, name fields in a similar manner. For forms and reports, name controls in a way to identify their function. Employing a consistent naming scheme for all aspects of the database design makes your database self-documenting.

- Keep written notes during the development process and produce a short "operator's manual" toward the final stages of construction. The developer notes will assist you and others in working on the database in the future while the operator's manual will help you see the database from the operator's perspective. Frequently, deficiencies in the user interface become apparent when you create an operator's manual.
- Use the built-in Access Database Documenter to generate a formal catalog of database objects. You can customize the output to include varying levels of detail about the objects you document.

How to Use the Access Database Documenter

Step 1.   Open the database you wish to document.

Step 2.   From the **Database Tools** ribbon, choose **Database Documenter** in the **Analyze** area.

Step 3.   Use the **Documenter** dialog box to select the desired objects to include in the documentation report. For each object class (tables, queries, forms, etc) you may use the **Options** button to specify the level of reporting detail.

Step 4.   Choose **OK** when done.

 The Object Documentation report will appear in **Print Preview**.

Appendix B | Creating a Workgroup Database

In this appendix, you will learn the skills necessary to split an Access database to permit workgroup distribution; distribute the database across a workgroup; and set workgroup database options.

What is a Workgroup Database?

A workgroup database is a database that may be accessed by several people concurrently, provided that the individual computers are on the same internal network and all have access to a common shared folder. As one person enters or edits records in a table, other people can see those changes almost immediately. Any and all edits done by individuals of the workgroup are updated almost immediately (there may be up to a minute delay) so the data in the database is truly shared. This represents a radical departure from working with a single database file. With a single file, only one person may have access to the data at a time (because the file is only available to one computer).. The following illustration shows a simple 3-computer arrangement.

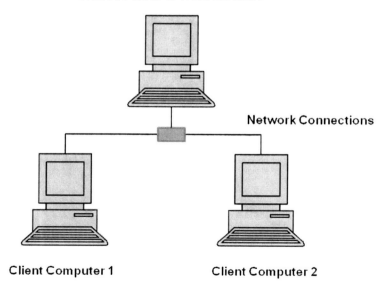

There are three major tasks to creating a workgroup database.

Task 1. Creating the Split Database

You begin will your original Access database. In the previous illustration, imagine that the database file resides on Client Computer 1. Your intent is to distribute your database so both Client Computer 1 and Client Computer 2 can access the data at the same time. Both the Client Computers must have Microsoft Access installed. The third computer, here labeled Shared Folder or Network Drive, will house the database back end, which is where the actual database tables in a split database reside. Note that Microsoft Access need not be installed on this shared computer.

The process begins by opening your original database file on Client Computer 1. You run the **Split Database Wizard** and when done, the Wizard moves the database tables to a file called the **backend** and places that file on the Shared Folder or Network Drive.

The **front end** file is essentially the original database file but with the tables removed to the new back end file. The front end file by default retains the name of the original database, although it can be renamed if desired. Although the **front** end lacks the tables, it maintains *links* to the original tables.

Task 2. Adjusting Workgroup Options

Any database workgroup options are set in the front end file. This step is optional.

Task 3. Distributing the Database Front End

Once the database has been split, you can copy the database file on Client Computer 1 to Client Computer 2, and indeed, to any other computer that has access to the back end file on the Shared Folder or Network Drive. Only the computers that host the front end file must have Microsoft Access installed.

If the back end file name is changed (*not recommended*) or if one of the workgroup computers uses an alias to refer to the shared folder, you will need to run the **Linked table manager** on the affected front end files. Refer to the next section for details.

How to Create a Split Database

You should run this procedure starting on one of the computers that has access to the shared network folder. When you use the **Database Splitter** you will indicate where the shared folder is in order to move the database back end file to that location. The front end file (containing everything but the original tables) will remain on the initial computer.

Step 1.   Create a backup copy of the original database file.

Step 2.   Start Access and open the original database file.

Step 3.   From the **Database Tools** ribbon, in the **Move Data** area, choose **Access Database**.

Step 4.   In the **Database Splitter** dialog box, choose **Split Database**.

Step 5.   In the **Create Back-end Database** dialog box, either accept the default name for the new back end file or type a new name in the **File name** box. Use the controls on the **Create Database Back-**End dialog to navigate to the shared folder, then choose **Split**.

The best practice is to name the back end using the front end (original) file name with the term *back end* appended to the file name.

Step 6.   Choose **OK** at the end of the splitting process.

How to Adjust the Database Workgroup Options

If you have just completed Step 6 from the previous procedure, you are in the original database file. It has had all tables moved to the new back end file created in Step 5. From this point forward, the original database file will be called the front end file. You may rename this file at some point if desired, but note that you cannot rename an open database file. You should use **Windows Explorer** to rename database files.

Step 1.   Open the front end file if necessary (this is not necessary if you have just completed the previous procedure).

Step 2.   From the **File** ribbon, choose **Options**.

Step 3.   Select the **Client Settings** control then scroll down to the **Advanced** area. Consult the following table for specific settings.

Workgroup Options

Option	Description
Default open mode	This property *must* be set to **Shared** (which is the default value).
Default record locking	These options establish how Access processes simultaneous edits from two or more users. The most efficient setting is **Edited Record**. **No locks** may permit two users to edit the same record without warning while **All records** completely locks a table from any edits by other users whenever someone begins editing data.
Open databases using record level locking	Check this option to force Access to protect only the current record being edited. Clearing this choice forces Access to protect a "page" of records at a time. You cannot predict which records constitutes a page.
Refresh Interval	This option designates the number of seconds between updates between the front and back end file. The default is 60 seconds. Choosing a lower number may affect database performance. Choosing a higher number increases performance but users must wait longer before seeing new or updated records.
Number of update retries	This is the number of times Access will attempt to save a changed record that is locked by another user.
Update retry interval (msec)	The time Access waits, in milliseconds, between update retries.

Step 4.   Adjust workgroup properties as desired. Note that not all the options on the **Advanced** tab relate directly to workgroup settings.

Step 5.   Choose **OK** to commit your changes or choose **Cancel** to close the dialog box without saving your changes.

How to Distribute the Database Front End

The database front end file is should be located on one of the computers that has access to the shared folder containing the database back end. Simply moving copies of the front end file to individual computers completes the task as long as each computer sees the same path to the shared folder. If a computer uses an alias to refer to the shared folder, or if the back end file name is changed (*not recommended*) you must use the **Linked Table Manger** to repair the broken link between the front and back end file.

Step 1.   From each destination computer, use **Windows Explorer** to create a copy of the front end file.

Step 2.   Locate a copy of the front end file on the local computer.

 It is a good practice to create a folder on the local computer to store the front end file. You may also wish to create a desktop shortcut to the database front end.

How to Work with a Workgroup Database

Step 1.   From one of the local computers, start Access and open the local copy of the front end file.

Step 2.   Use the database as usual.

 Warning: Editing records in a workgroup database will make the edited record unavailable to other workgroup users for editing (but not for viewing). Keep editing time to a minimum and do not leave the database in edit mode for extended periods of time.

 The **Refresh Interval** setting (discussed above) controls how often a front end file synchronizes with the common back end file. For applications where several users are making frequent changes to the database you may wish to adjust this setting to a smaller (more frequent updates) value.

Mending Broken Links

If the back end file name is changed (*not recommended*) or if one of the workgroup computers uses an alias to refer to the shared folder, you will need to run the **Linked** table manager on the affected front end files.

The **Linked Table Manager** is a wizard that reestablishes the link between any given front end and the back end file. Two points to consider:

- You must know the name and location of the back end file to proceed.

- The computer you are working on must be able to access the shared folder that contains the back end file.

How to Use the Linked Table Manager

Step 1.   From the computer whose front end file cannot "see" the back end file, open the front end file.

Step 2.	From the **External Data** ribbon, in the **Import & Link** area, choose **Linked Table Manager**.
Step 3.	In the **Linked Table Manager**, place a check in the **Always prompt for new location** checkbox.
Step 4.	Choose **Select All**.
Step 5.	Choose **OK**.
Step 6.	In the **Select New Location of** (*back end file name*) dialog box, navigate to the location of the back end file and select the file. Choose **Open** when done.
Step 7.	At the end of the linking process, choose **OK** to finish.

Appendix C | Staff and Projects Database

The samples in this manual illustrate a simple staff and projects database – a design that might commonly be used in an organization that tracks information about staff (contact methods and skills) as well as information about projects (here the main interest is in the staffing of projects as well as the budget for a project). A copy of this database may be downloaded from www.sycamoretechnicalpress.com

The basic relationships between the tables used in the sample database appear in the following illustration.

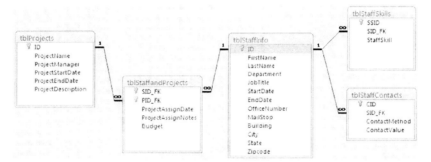

The structure of the 5 tables, and if applicable, the indices used to maintain uniqueness among rows, are presented below.

tblStaffInfo

This table, along with tblProjects, can be considered the two main tables in the staff and projects database. A primary key affords an easy way to relate a staff record to other tables and an index based on staff first and last name as well as department enforce uniqueness for each row.

Field Name	Data Type	Description
ID	AutoNumber	Primary Key
FirstName	Text	
LastName	Text	
Department	Text	
JobTitle	Text	
StartDate	Date/Time	
EndDate	Date/Time	
OfficeNumber	Text	
MailStop	Text	
Building	Text	
City	Text	

There are two indices for tblStaffInfo. The primary key is automatically created by Access. The index **Staff** asserts that no two records may contain the same staff first and last name and department.

tblProjects

Along with tblStaffInfo this table constitutes the other major table in the Staff and Projects database. Both tables store information about the two realms the database focuses on. Like the tblStaffInfo table, a second index **Project** enforces uniqueness by assuming the combination of project name, project manager, and start date will not be repeated.

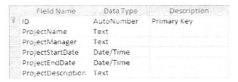

The indexes for tblProjects appears as:

tblStaffContact

This table relates the one-to-many ways you can contact each staff member. An index based on the foreign key for the staff ID, the contact method, and the contact value, ensure that no two rows are duplicated.

Field Name	Data Type	Description
CID	AutoNumber	Primary Key
SID_FK	Number	Foreign key to tblStaffInfo Primary Key
ContactMethod	Text	
ContactValue	Text	

The index appears as follows:

tblStaffSkills

Similar to tblStaffContacts, this table stores any skills associated with each staff member.

Field Name	Data Type	Description
SSID	AutoNumber	
SID_FK	Number	Foreign key to tblStaffInfo Primary Key
StaffSkill	Text	

The index, based on the staff foreign key and staff skill, ensures uniqueness for each row:

tblStaffandProjects

The final table is the only bridge table in this design. It's purpose is to manage the information that relates to project staffing. Each project may have one or more staff assigned to it, and ultimately, each staff member may be assigned to zero or more projects. It is also the only table in the database design to utilize two fields which together make up the table's primary key: the foreign key to the tblStaffInfo primary key and the foreign key to the tblProjects primary key. Using these two fields together ensures uniqueness among the rows and enforces the logical requirement that no staff can be assigned to a project more than once. This simple design removes any requirement for an additional index to enforce uniqueness among the records.

Further, in this design the budget field implies that each staff member is given an individual budget for their part in a project. Recall from the discussion on banded reports that even given this configuration, with a project staffed by several members from the same department, one can easily generate a report that groups project staffing information by department, with the purpose of providing totals of the budget amount both by staff, by department, and by project.

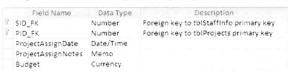

Field Name	Data Type	Description
SID_FK	Number	Foreign key to tblStaffInfo primary key
PID_FK	Number	Foreign key to tblProjects primary key
ProjectAssignDate	Date/Time	
ProjectAssignNotes	Memo	
Budget	Currency	

Index

About the Author

F. Mark Schiavone was originally trained as a research scientist, and in that capacity he began constructing database applications and analyzing complex data sets over 30 years ago. His database skills include Microsoft Access, Microsoft SQL Server and MySQL and he has constructed applications using those platforms for clients in large to mid-size organizations, including the US Department of Education, the National Weather Service, and the International Monetary Fund. He has authored over 30 training titles in topics such as Microsoft Access, Microsoft Word, Microsoft Excel, and in the VBA programming language. Each of these titles were designed with the busy technology worker in mind and focus on important and useful tasks.

Along with his partner John he has restored three stone houses (two of which were 18th century while the most recent house dates from 1835), reroofed a loafing barn, disassembled and reassembled a corn crib, and built several frame houses, additions or outbuildings. He has designed every new structure built on their property. He is a passionate all weather, high mileage motorcyclist and is usually the only motorcyclist on the local roads when the temperature is below 25° F.

Cover Design: Martha A. Loomis

CPSIA information can be obtained
at www.ICGtesting.com
Printed in the USA
LVOW09s0303030217
523119LV00004B/322/P